The Ride Home

KEITH HURST

BACK ROADS PUBLISHING

Scripture quotations in this publication are taken from the Holy Bible, translations as follows:

NIV: Scripture quotations marked (NIV) are taken from the Holy Bible, New International
Version®, NIV®. Copyright ©1973, 1978, 1984, 2011 by Biblica, Inc.™ Used by permission
of Zondervan. All rights reserved worldwide. www.zondervan.com, The "NIV" and "New
International Version" are trademarks registered in the United States Patent and Trademark
Office by Biblica, Inc.™

GW: GOD'S WORD is a copyrighted work of God's Word to the Nations. Quotations are
used by permission. Copyright 1995 by God's Word to the Nations. All rights reserved.

ESV: Scripture quotations marked (ESV) are from The Holy Bible, English Standard Version®
(ESV®), copyright ©2001 by Crossway, a publishing ministry of Good News Publishers. Used
by permission. All rights reserved.

Library of Congress Catalog-In-Publication Number: 2017918698
ISBN: 978-1979078290
CreateSpace Independent Publishing Platform, North Charleston, SC

Front and back cover photos by Angel Dawn Stewart Photography.
Cover and interior design by Machele Brass of Brass Design.

Printed in the United States of America.

BACK ROADS PUBLISHING

Dedication

This book is dedicated to my family.

To my wife, Dana: Simply, you are the reason I try. You are the reason I get up every morning and face the day. You believe in me even when I struggle to believe in myself. You are the Yin to my Yang, the Rock to my Roll, or in my case...the Country to my Western. You have been there to lift my spirits for over twenty years. You are never short on opinions on how we could improve, which expands my thinking. You are a fabulous mother, wife and friend. I am so happy that Rick Deviney bugged me to no end to go to the beginning-of-the-year get-together back at UAM that fateful night. It, along with you, changed my life. Thanks, and I love you.

To my daughter, Hannah: Your tireless desire to be the best God has called you to be is a true inspiration. You always put others before yourself, and you are a perfect example of how servant leaders should conduct themselves. You made parenting easier than it probably should have been. You lead by example, encourage the downtrodden, and shine your quiet leadership brightly. Each step you take leaves an everlasting footprint for others to follow. I am overjoyed that God blessed me by allowing us to be family. You are amazing, beautiful, and thoughtful. Thank you. Dad loves you.

To my son, Hayden: You are a typical teenage boy, as you should be, but when it comes to what really matters in life—like standing up for others who can't fend for themselves, our family, and, most importantly, Christ—you are spot on. You make me proud every day. When you were born, my life changed. You made me strive to be the best example of how a godly man should be. I wanted to be an example you could point to, not run from. I watched as you applied God's principles in the hardest of times, like taking the high road and turning the other cheek when your "flesh" said to do the opposite. God recognized it, as did I. Keep your commitment to your commitments; be willing to fail and use mistakes as growth opportunities. You have greatness within you. Hold yourself to high standards and, when you decide, buckle your seatbelt because you will experience some rough roads before the black-top, but it will all be worth it. I love you, son.

To my mom, Mary Hurst: Thank you. You were the perfect mother for me. You had to be both mom and dad, and you filled those roles well. You taught me by example, and I learned by observing you. At age nine, I listened as you talked to a friend who needed money to feed her four kids. I watched as you took your last twenty dollars (and borrowed another twenty from a neighbor) and gave it all to your friend. Then you went out mowed three yards and gave the borrowed money back. You taught me how to give unselfishly and to put others first. Little lessons like those were sprinkled all throughout my younger years and helped form the person I am today. Thank you for being true to who you are and being the best and brightest example of a quiet servant leader. If I can parent my kids half as well as you did me, then I will have been a success. Thanks, mom. I love you.

To Jesus: Thank You for saving me, for Your sacrifice, for Your endless examples of kindness and leadership. I know sometimes You must look down at me and think to Yourself, "Are you *serious*? Will that boy ever learn?" but I am grateful for Your forgiveness. You have always provided for my family, and for that I am particularly thankful. You have stood in the gap for us, guided us in our darkest times, and laughed with us as we enjoyed sweet victories. You are my True North. Thank You for "checking me" when I need it, straightening out my curves, and offering Your gentle hand when I need help up. You are my Hero.

Table of Contents

Acknowledgements

I would like to acknowledge a few people who have impacted my life over the years.

God, from Whom all blessing flow. Thanks for being the compass for us to follow, and for providing direction and compassion. Each time I fail, I can always look up and know that I am forgiven.

All of my former coaches who took the time and "bled" into me over the years: P.E. "Bubba" Boney, "Dandy" Don Lenderman, Jerry White, and Robert Williams. Each one of you helped mold me into the man I am today.

One very special man—my very first coach, Doug Riley. You knew my situation from the very start. Thank you for the countless rides to and from practice and games over the years (not to mention the rides home during lunch hour so Mike and I could watch "All My Children" while we ate). Your constant encouragement changed my life. You took a fatherless boy and helped him grow into a man. You never knew, but I watched as you fathered Marty and Mike and, secretly, I envied those bonds. Thanks for allowing me to join in when you played catch in the street with your boys, for challenging me to catch that nasty knuckle ball you always threw, and for verbally kicking my butt when I dropped out of college that one semester. You taught me that coaching isn't just about Xs and Os but rather about building belief where there once was none. It's about developing character and reaching back and helping others along the way. It's about making a difference, one person at a time. You never knew it, but you were my role model and template that I followed as I tried to parent my kids. A simple "thank you" doesn't seem sufficient.

Pastor Casey Henagan (PC), who welcomed us and provided a place for our family to worship. You seem to always be speaking directly to me as you teach. Keypoint Church has been a major blessing to our family and others, and it's because you allow God to lead you and use you and Stacy for the betterment of mankind. Thanks for being the example for others to follow and for standing firm in your convictions. Your work has had and will continue to have a major impact on northwest Arkansas and beyond. God bless, PC.

All my former athletes with whom I had the pleasure of working and coaching: My prayer is that I was able to leave more with you than just some knowledge of the game. You each presented me with a wonderful and unique challenge, and I learned way more by coaching you than ya'll ever learned from me. It was fun. I am equally grateful to your parents, who entrusted you to the coaching staff. Thank you for knowing your role and performing it flawlessly. You each are an unsung hero.

NWA Legendary Sports Organization and NWA Legends Teams: It was awesome to be affiliated with such a caring organization. I was always proud to wear the red, white, and black and sport the Legends logo. What an amazing group of players, coaches, and parents! I'm truly blessed to be a part of what continues to grow.

Lance Nations, thank you for bugging the crap out of me to help. I am so glad you did. If you hadn't, this book would never have been written. You did amazing things with our teams and took them to heights that some thought were impossible. You are an amazing coach and a fantastic father and husband. You continue to research and learn, which is the mark of a true professional. Stacy Nations, thanks for all you did to help Lance get the organization started and thanks for keeping it running. I will miss asking you the score every half-inning just to see if you would ignore me or not. HA!!

NWA Legends 99: You girls helped me find my coaching joy again. You forced me to grow daily to try and lead by example. Thanks for listening to my impromptu "life talks" in the hotel rooms, on the fields, in the dugout, and in the vehicle (like ya'll had a choice!). Sorry for all the off-the-cuff music trivia at what seemed to be the weirdest of times. For every kid who wore the red, white, and black, I hope you left better than when you came. You each are special and flawless, and I appreciate you all.

Special thanks to Karen Sjoblom: Your editing skills are ON POINT! You took the ramblings of a small town country boy and made them more than comprehensible. You are amazing at your craft. You have a huge and open heart and it shows in your writing. Thank you for taking my life's work and arranging it in such a way that others may experience what we feel. God shows up and shows out in your work. Thank you so much for taking on my project and believing in it from the very start. I appreciate you and your talents.

Preface

It was a cool, brisk, late November afternoon while sitting in a tree stand deep in the Delta hardwoods when my thoughts turned to the previous summer's team. Coaching has always been something that feeds my soul, and I was recognizing the memories would be a way to brace for the cold, dismal winter that was sure to hit our small northwest Arkansas town. Baseball, softball and football take me back to my own childhood, my children's childhoods, and the times when I could forget all my responsibilities and just get lost in the sweetness of the game. But after those quarters and innings, it was always the ride home that opened up new vistas to me. Something as simple as passing the miles while talking about faith and leadership has, I've found, impacted more players than I could have ever known. And it seemed to me if these kids were remembering these brief snatches of time so deeply, well, maybe we all should listen in.

I wrote this book to share what I think is the beautiful simplicity of a game of ball, and the equally beautiful complexity of the life lessons surrounding it. As with many things, there's so much more to learn below the obvious surface, and I found those long rides home to be a sweet and colorful canvas on which to spread my ideas on living well. It's my belief it really does take a village to raise our kids, and I have been so proud and grateful to be asked to pour into this next generation of leaders. Over my many years of coaching, I've learned how humans respond to both praise and challenge, and that it's equally important to nurture feelings as well as skills.

I find myself hard-wired to encourage and uplift...to make sure that others know they were born to win in life, and not just in games. Helping others discover their talents, strengthen their faith, and build on their commitments is paramount. While some act out their calling in board rooms, mine has been honed in locker rooms and on ball fields, in hotel meeting rooms and in dugouts. Over thousands of miles and too many innings to count, I've gotten the gift of living out my calling while helping develop and encourage our next generation of leaders.

While most people judge success by wins and losses, I believe true success is found in honest relationships and learning, in being open to failing, in keeping our commitments and in having uncompromising standards. Simply put, true success is being happy with how you live… and how your life has turned out. But the truth is, while it took a while to gain this wisdom, I learned all the lessons I ever really needed on those rides home.

LEGENDS 99 HEADING TO A TOURNAMENT IN STARKVILLE, MS

Chapter One

ON LESSONS THAT LAST

It's been said that life lessons can be learned any number of ways. For me, it seems most of the lessons I recall revolved around sporting events and ballgames. The bulk of my education didn't come from school, or a father figure, because I grew up without one. My education came from those long, quiet, thought-filled nights sitting in the back of a yellow school bus. Those nights heading home with my teammates were priceless: Our conversations ranged from how we played that night to our families, futures, relationships, and lessons learned.

We had it all figured out, or so we thought.

The lessons that stuck the most weren't necessarily about the competition, even though winning and losing are filled with teachable moments. The truth is, I learned the most by observing others—how they reacted, and interacted. I've often wondered why people act the way they do...what motivates someone to be kind or cruel to another. But back in the day, while my teammates laughed and joked, my thoughts centered on how I'd acted and reacted, what I could have done better, which plays might have changed the outcome. And of course, the hopeful part of me wondered who saw me play, what they thought, and whether my name would be in tomorrow's paper.

You see, while autumn Friday nights are special all over, we Southerners seem to take them to rather lofty levels. Entire volumes and television shows have been created around the love for our teams, and Friday nights in the stands are a type of religion, our way of life. But even after all these years, one particular Friday evening memory flickers back to life every time summer wanes.

It was early November, gloomy and soggy. The rain seemed to have been falling for several days, starting on a Wednesday and pelting our small, southeast Arkansas town until early Friday. Picture it: A couple of minutes left in a 0-0 game, a muddy field, and a rain-soaked football thrown in a somewhat tight spiral, perfectly placed to a receiver (me) who's two full yards ahead of his closest defensive back as he crosses the end zone in triumph.

Now: This is what dreams are made of—what young boys think about in their backyards while tossing a football into the air, watching carefully as it falls ever so lightly back into their hands and reveling in cheers only they can hear. It's making that grab, winning the game, being lifted onto your teammates' shoulders because that catch meant an undefeated season.

The moment of a young lifetime.

Did I mention the ball was perfectly placed? Our quarterback heaved it over fifty-five yards through the heavy night air, right into the waiting arms of his receiver (remember, me)...only to watch it slip in painfully slow motion through a pair of outstretched hands and hydroplane through the back of the end zone. It was like a scene straight out of the movie *The Best of Times* with Robin Williams and Kurt Russell in which such a play is redeemed several years later, deciding once and for all: Hero or the goat.

Those forty yards back to the sidelines were probably the longest I'd ever walked, seeing the disappointment on the coaches' faces after calling the perfect play, hearing the fans moan in disgust, and watching the punt team jog onto the spongy field to kick yet another ball on another failed opportunity. It was unbelievably tough to stomach, but it proved to be a valuable moment in my life that revisits me every so often. I grew up a little that night.

We won that game after three overtimes, eventually scoring a whopping three points and reaching our goal of an undefeated season. But what I remember the most is standing alone at midfield, watching everyone else celebrate. I stood both within and without the celebrating, in and out of time, knowing something big had taken place but not yet being able to articulate (much less appreciate) it. Some major life lessons were pounded into me that night, but I didn't realize their full value until about twenty years later—like learning when life knocks you down seven times, you need to get up eight. That just because you failed doesn't make you a failure, and just because you lose doesn't make you a loser.

I learned there is no shame in getting knocked down. The only shame is if you stay down.

In my work and my life, I have shared some of these hard-won lessons with many athletes, friends, couples, singles, non-athletes, employees, employers, and business owners. My intention always has been to share them freely with whoever's willing to listen in hopes that each would pay it forward. Such lessons are both common and rare; with them, I believe we can help lift one another and do our part to make the world a better place.

I am hard-wired to be an encourager: My dream has always been to build belief in others and let them know that they are unique. I help people identify their God-given gifts and talents, and am grateful to play a small part in showing how to apply what was entrusted to them. I long to let others know that God has plans for their lives, and that as much as we like to think we orchestrate them, we don't. God does. I believe life is filled with teaching moments if we are open to receive them: If life is going to happen regardless, why not be willing to learn along the way? Just as in life, this book is filled with victories and defeats, wins and losses, joys and sorrows. The amazing fact is we can learn from each one—the good and the hard—and that knowledge shapes our character which, in turn, reveals the person we were always supposed to become.

As an adult, I had been involved in coaching various aspects of baseball or softball for around twenty years by the time I met Coach Lance Nations. He was putting together a 13U travel softball team, but he was a little late to the table when it came to hosting tryouts, if you know what I mean. Late, like, it was *late January*, and most teams had formed a few months prior and already were practicing for the spring season that was set to start in early March. By the time he started scouting, as we say down here in the South, "The pickins' were slim." When it came to finding top-notch talent, especially for a team with no history to fall back on, the Coach was at a loss.

Lance put together a rag-tag team that would have made the Bad News Bears look positively trophy-worthy. I was looking forward to re-signing myself to the stands, to just being a dad who toted lawn chairs and dragged ice chests to the ball park. But apparently, God had a different plan.

Let me just say I had no intention of coaching my daughter. I love her to death, but it can be very difficult for all parties when a player is coached by a parent. You have to be mindful of neither taking it too easy or too hard on them, balancing between playing "daddy ball" versus benching them more than the others for fear of playing favorites. It can be a very fine line…a line that Lance never crossed, by the way. He set the standards and the expectations right from the start, and he did exactly what he said he would do…though he never, outright, admitted to finagling a certain someone into coaching. But then, after several attempts to get me to assist and just as many refusals, he convinced me to join him in the dugout for one game. And somehow, without my knowledge, I ended up back out on the field a short time later.

Looking back, I am very thankful he was persuasive, wearing me down for the best of reasons. From this sweet second chance, I've revisited the old memories, and the more recent ones, remembering the lessons that came from being a player and a coach, and weaving together something that hopefully captures the best of sport, and life. **The Ride Home** is a very special story of hope and disappointment, encouragement and overcoming. It chronicles the journey of a special group of athletes, coaches and parents. I hope to bring to life the lessons taught and learned by all involved, especially mine.

During those rides home from tryouts in my youth, conversations revolved around discerning God's plan and being open to accepting it. It can be difficult putting yourself out there in a new situation of any kind, but it's especially hard when you are thirteen. I remember we talked about courage, and how it isn't necessarily running into a burning building to save people (although that is a fantastic example). Somehow we figured that courage is simply doing what your heart tells you to do, even when it's hard, even when no one applauds. Sometimes it's standing by your commitments when everyone else is following the crowd. Sometimes it's eating in the lunch room alone instead of hanging with others who make questionable decisions. Sometimes it's welcoming the kid who desperately needs a friend, and sometimes it's putting others far ahead of ourselves.

We didn't necessarily know the full extent of life's courage then; there was no way we could. But in the many years since those bittersweet autumn evenings, I've found courage is simply being **OK** with who you are, and knowing, more importantly, Whose you are.

HAYDEN MID-GAME

Chapter Two

ON STAYING IN THE GAME

In travel ball, part of the pain of losing is purely financial because it's such an expensive sport. First, there's the initial cost of joining an organization, which can run from $250 to $1,200 or more per season (and two seasons per year). Second, there's the equipment: $400 for bats (most kids "need" two), $300 to $400 for catcher's gear, and so much more. Third, there's the cost to attend the approximately seven hundred games per season—with parents and coaches taking off early from work on most Fridays, gas money, hotel stays, food and snacks and drinks both on and off the field. Fourth, there are the overpriced t-shirts. Everyone knows you must purchase at least two t-shirts per tournament, one for the player and another one for the parent. (Or, one for dusting and one for cleaning your rims eventually, depending on how you look at it.) The shirt shack is usually the first place players and parents stop when they enter; quite fortuitously, it's placed conveniently just beside the entrance to catch folks while there's still money in their wallets. Some parents justify these purchases by saying they're going to make a quilt out of the shirts when their players have "retired". They know, even as they speak, that quilt will never materialize, but still…all the hopes and memories will remain, captured in those faded cotton blends.

And fifth: In Arkansas, softball tournaments for the most part are three-game guarantees, which means if you want to play more than three games in any given weekend, you'd better win at least once.

For that one season of ours in particular, this seemed to be the place where we were falling down a bit.

Losing, by itself, is difficult for anyone to swallow, but factor in an extra $500 or more per weekend and a normally mild-mannered person can become practically rabid, chomping at the bit to win at any cost. I can still recall that disheartening conversation between Coach Lance and I when we were arguing gently over whether we'd lost seventeen or eighteen games, and whether that had happened over five or six tournaments.

It should not have been lost on us that, at some point, such numbers no longer matter.

The ultimate message was painfully clear: Something had to change.

* * *

Back in the day, it seemed all of our softball dads were named James but, in reality, there were only three. Still, three out of eleven is more than most teams would have, I guess, and it made remembering these men that much simpler. All joking aside, we were blessed with a truly unforgettable group of parents that season, and everyone became friends rather quickly. It was by design, really: Lance and I, along with our spouses, Stacy and Dana, believed we needed to interview the parents just as much if not more than the players. We knew that for us to accomplish what we set out to do, we had to have a spectacular supporting cast. Each person bought into our philosophy of Positive Coaching and Hustle, and each understood the process.

Now, a good coach usually has a few "go-to" talks when it comes to addressing a team after a loss. That season, I believe we exhausted every single one…and even recycled a few. Eighteen straight losses? What can one say that hasn't already been said? We knew we needed a new approach and a different message.

Years ago while attending Keypoint Church in Springdale, Arkansas, I'd heard Pastor Casey (PC) give a talk on facing a crisis, saying that those hard places can be one of two things—either a birthplace or a graveyard for your faith. This message hit home with me and I've never forgotten it. When we face challenges of any kind, we have to lean on

God's promises, and there are over 3,000 to choose from in the Bible. We also have to remember God's character—His power, His love, His trustworthiness and faithfulness. We must focus on what God has done for us and believe He can and will do it again. In fact, Jesus Himself said, "As far as possibilities go, everything is possible for the person who believes" (Mark 9:23, GW). This message is still true today. It doesn't matter what your situation is; even if your life is in chaos, His Word is true, and He will not go back on His promises.

Furthermore, inspirational author Orison Swett Marden suggested that success is far less about our accomplishments and far more about the courage we exhibit when faced with great opposition. I learned this first during that long-ago autumn game, and knew we needed to apply this wisdom to our struggling team if we wanted to turn things around.

Toward that end, Lance focused more on drills—drill after drill after drill: his gifting. I worked on technique and what I do best, which is uplifting and motivating people. Every coach must know their strengths and be diligent about identifying their weaknesses. On a scale from 1 to 10, when it comes to teaching the art of hitting, I would give myself a 4…maybe a 5 if I am feeling generous. It is not my strong suit. But apply the same scale to my fielding, and I would rate myself an 8 or a 9. I enjoy teaching the technique, the footwork, the positioning and, most of all, the mindset.

And while hitting and fielding are vital when it comes to competing, I believe those take a back seat to the mental approach, the psychology of it all. So let's take the same scale and apply it to the psychological approach to the game. If a coach understands and utilizes this approach, he can get a player with a belief level of a 5 and a talent level of a 7 to play at a 9 or a 10 consistently. The psychological aspect is my favorite part of coaching by far, and it's how I spend the majority of my study time and where I would rate myself as the most beneficial. I have spent countless hours studying why people act the way they do as well as what influences them. I have been blessed to empower athletes to perform far better than their confidence and ability alone should ever allow. It has nothing to do with technique and everything to do with building belief and relaying positive affirmations. In other words, it's what Lance and I call "Positive Coaching," meaning we correct in a positive manner, discipline in private, and praise in public.

After over twenty years of working with young athletes on the ins and outs of baseball and softball, coaching is, in my opinion, way more than technique, footwork and bunt coverage. It is more than outfield placement and knowing which pitch to call. Don't get me wrong; all of these things are very important to the success of an athlete and a team but, to me, coaching is about *making a difference*. It's about building belief in players where there once was none, and planting enough encouragement so they know they have what it takes to stay in the game—of ball *and* of life.

If coaches (or parents, for that matter) would make reading a habit, lives would be changed—theirs and those around them. I believe this with all my heart. If coaches could relate to each player in a more personal, relevant manner, they would elevate each teammate to a level they only dreamed of. And if a coach read two books and applied what he or she learned, their players would reach new heights in their performance as well as their attitudes…and the coach would become better at their craft by default.

I became an avid reader back in 2004; until then, I had never read an entire book from front to back. As a matter of fact, I confess I hated to read, but I wanted a change in my life and my lifestyle, to be a positive example for my wife and kids and not a roadblock. So, I focused at first on my topics of interest: relationship, self-help, personality and spiritual books. I'd heard somewhere to develop a lasting habit, one should do that new behavior for at least twenty-one days straight. Thus, I focused on committing to read a minimum of fifteen pages each night, no exceptions. I then applied that knowledge to my relationships, my work and my coaching. I learned that much of a player's success or failure was in how I approached each one. I learned to first make sure they knew I cared for them as people, not just athletes. I also needed to convey that it wasn't all about me, but all about them, which allowed me to break down walls and barriers quickly. And once that was established, my players could become far more receptive to my coaching, their confidence increasing along with their performance and productivity.

Toward this end, the two books I recommend to all coaches are **Personality Plus** and **The 5 Love Languages**, neither of which has anything to do with athletics, but everything to do with everything else. After reading **Personality Plus**, a coach would be more in tune with their players' personalities and what makes each one of them tick. That same coach would soon realize that saying one thing to a particular player to get them excited enough to run through a wall could shut down a different player altogether.

If a coach doesn't understand his or her players' personality types and what motivates or stunts them, the player-coach relationship can be very rocky. My other top choice, **The 5 Love Languages**, talks about the different ways people feel loved, special and wanted. I will refrain from listing all the love languages here because I believe this book should be read in full several times over, but will give an example. Maybe one player's love language is *Words of Affirmation*, meaning positive messages and praise are the greatest motivators. Once a coach identifies this particular love language, he or she then just needs to find and affirm the things the player does well. It could be as simple as saying "Great job!" or "Your technique was on point today". Even telling such players that you're proud of them can make all the difference in their confidence which, in turn, will boost their play.

It seems nowadays that coaches don't feel the need to get to know their players, or they default to dealing with everyone in the same way. I call this the "old school method" in which a coach expects the players to conform to his or her way only—*my way or the highway*. But I believe that learning a bit about each player's personality and love language, and coaching to *those*, can take the team, the player *and* the coach to new heights.

Finally, I've noticed that sometimes coaches are so focused on winning that their athletes suffer, because that's their sole emphasis rather than bringing out the best in each player. For Coach Lance and me, we learned that when our players *knew* we honestly cared for them more than winning, we got their best at all times.

On that long ride home after loss number eighteen, we talked about applying our new philosophy and about keeping the faith. In fact, we discussed using faith as a reference point, an anchor...something on which we can always depend, no matter the situation. I shared what I'd learned at a prayer breakfast from a former Arkansas Razorback basketball coach on some truths in life: He said there will always be a battle, but we have a chance to prove daily how tough we are physically and mentally. Lance and I talked about obedience, and how partial obedience is disobedience, and about setting boundaries in life and keeping them. We committed to doing what is right, especially when it is hard, and about helping our players choose their friends carefully—friends who could support rather than squash their dreams. We determined to be other-centered servant leaders, planting in our young players' fields hope and encouragement and possibilities.

That "losing" weekend was a turning point, and soon after things started to click.

In a blackly comical twist, we traveled to Kansas City that following weekend and lost the next game, which took us to an epic 0-19, but the very next match up brought us the breakthrough for which we were hoping and working and praying. Winning that first game, you would have thought we triumphed at the World Series for all the celebrating and fist-pumping that took place. In the end, Kansas City turned out to be a very special place for our group—a place not only known for its outstanding barbeque, but one where our players (and their coaches) found their true voices and vocations.

By discerning and implementing these changes, and committing to knowing our players, we grew their confidence and our own to boot... just by staying in the game.

The changes became evident. And it was marvelous to behold.

LEX AND AJ AFTER THEIR TWO COLLEGE TEAMS PLAYED AGAINST EACH OTHER

Chapter Three

ON LEARNING AND TEACHING

How is it that when an athlete plays for one coach, he or she will play "lights out," but when they perform for a different coach, it's a struggle? Let's look at high school versus competitive travel ball. The competition level is about the same; as a matter of fact, in most cases, it's *stronger* during the summer months than the school year because of teams combining and cherry-picking the better players from surrounding towns. They hold tryouts and put together all-star players at each position and take to the field playing against similarly populated teams.

The game doesn't change: It's still seven innings and nine players—a pitcher, a catcher, three outfielders, and four infielders.

The geography doesn't change: For the most part, they're the exact fields the players trod just a week earlier.

The only thing that differs is *the coach, the coaching, and the philosophy*.

So, you can take a kid who has a batting average between .400 and .500, who is a solid defender during the summer months (a.k.a. travel ball season), and put him or her on another high school team and watch the performance drop to levels you can't comprehend. It's stunning, confusing, and downright frustrating. Mind you, this isn't a knock on high school versus travel ball, but rather is more about one philosophy versus another.

Maybe you've seen the same thing over the years. Why is this? I'll share a thought that's both illuminating and humbling: I don't coach now the way I did when I was in my twenties or even my thirties. When I was new to the game, I coached kids the way I was coached: *old school*.

Old school rules said *never praise, always criticize*. We didn't hear when we did something right, but we (and everyone else in the stands) heard plenty when we screwed up. But as I grew and matured in my own coaching, I often thought back and wondered what it might have been like to have had a coach with a more positive disposition—a coach who critiqued in private and praised in public, who knew how to build belief in his players instead of chipping away at a fragile foundation. Some might read this and think it's too soft of an approach, but I believe it to be innovative. Why not explore ways to bring out the best in others?

I think the biggest issue, back when I was very green in the coaching ranks, was that I didn't understand certain elements of the human psyche. One of my most talented teams, in fact, was the very first team I ever coached. We had great ballplayers at every position—it was a coach's dream. I was eager to prove myself, but I didn't understand how to bring out the best in others. It sounds so elementary now, but I didn't realize each player had a unique personality that would react differently to my coaching style. I could say the same thing to three different players, and one would be excited, one would shut down, and one would let it pass in one ear and out the other. In other words, I didn't fully comprehend how words and tone affect people differently. Those boys should have won two or three state titles before they were done, except I was not a very good coach to them at the time. For that, I've been truly sorry. I think I've apologized to each one individually a few times over the years. They have been gracious to their old coach: We've laughed and chosen to remember the good times, but honestly? It still eats at me.

I started to see several of my shortcomings at the age of thirty-four, and that's when my coaching philosophy changed. I became an avid reader to learn how to bring out the best in others. Who knew that my academic nemesis while attending the University of Arkansas at Monticello—Psychology 101—would prove to be my saving grace...not only in coaching, but in relationships with friends, family and co-workers?

It wasn't easy; I took and either failed or dropped that class three or four times. It wasn't until I treated my professor to a crawfish boil, a few cold adult beverages, and a long levy ride that I was able to convince him how badly I needed to pass his class. I finally squeaked by with a C: I've never been so happy to be considered "average". (It's amazing what a little Southern hospitality can do to bring down the barriers between a Yankee and a Delta boy; there is something special about leaving the black top with the windows down, Merle Haggard easing his way out of the radio and spinning tires against gravel, that helps one man understand another man's plight.)

I don't remember anything else from my college classes, but what interests me most now is why people act and say the things they do. In other words, *psychology*. If this doesn't show God's sense of humor, I don't know what will.

Poet Maya Angelou suggested once we know better, we do better. So now, as a coach, I remind my players that they were, and are, flawless—that our God doesn't make mistakes. My commission is to lay a strong foundation for my athletes, so that when life throws an overhand right to their jaws, they know they are equipped to handle it and can build from it. God put them in my care for that particular reason, for that particular season, and I don't take that lightly.

I know better, so I do better.

I wanted to write this chapter because I am watching a similar situation unfold with two of my players. Both of these players—one baseball, one softball—are amazing kids. They love the game when they are with me in travel ball, but I have watched their affection wane over the past two years due to their high school experiences. I am not saying my way is the be-all-end-all or even close to the best, but I have seen firsthand that the things I've learned over the years and applied to the game tend to benefit *all* of us. When they play for me, both athletes are amazing at their craft, extremely confident at the plate as well as in the field. I have focused on building my players' confidence and belief systems along with their technique and footwork. I have had those hard conversations when needed, but they are done in private and in such a way as to edify and not demean.

So, I ask again: How can some teammates play their hearts out against better competitors for one coach and then struggle to make the

17

field and garner playing time with another?

The only explanation, in my opinion, is the difference in the philosophy of their coaches. Their talent hasn't changed, the game is the same, and the bases are similar in length. I have been able to get marginal players to sign letters of intent to further their ball-playing careers into college while more talented players on other teams don't play past high school. It has less to do with technique, batting stance, and hours of practice (even though those are important) and more to do with confidence and knowing someone believes in them. The simple truth is, my players play better because I believe they can...an*d I make sure they know it.* They aren't afraid to make a mistake, because they know I am ok with missteps as long as they are giving their best effort. They play loose for me because of how they are treated; I expect the best from them, and I get it every time. They know when a mistake is made, we'll talk about it...but they also get praised, too, which seems to be lacking in sports these days.

If I had to note some differences with these two players in high school ball, it's that their whole demeanor changes; they play tight, not free, if they even get the opportunity to play at all. They're afraid if they make a mistake they won't get another chance to showcase their abilities. Their coaches don't seem to care much; it's just a job, and it shows. It almost seems as though they've forgotten why they got into coaching in the first place. I bet if you polled young coaches today and asked why they chose to be in that role, you'd likely hear they wanted to make a difference. But sadly, as the years go by, that desire can fade for some reason.

From what I have seen, many coaches don't seem to care much for the psychology of the game; it's more about winning and losing, Xs and Os. But if that's the case, they're missing out on being able to make *a true and lasting impact* that could affect generations to come. The research I've done by talking to hundreds of softball and baseball players has led me to conclude that most players don't feel their coaches actually care for them as human beings. This is so unfortunate, and so very sad, *and so easily remedied.* If today's coaches would read some great books and put their newfound knowledge to work, it would impact them, their families, their players, their communities—*all* their relationships would be strengthened.

On a side note, those two ball players might never grace the field of a varsity high school game again, but that's OK. One has already signed her national letter of intent to play softball in college, and the other will also play ball in college but the sport will be his choice. They will take with them the invaluable lessons they've learned, thereby knowing (and doing) better.

In sports or in life, we can learn from everyone and anyone—what to do and what not to do. We can learn how to treat others and, more importantly, how not to treat them. I have instilled these truths in each player I've had the pleasure of coaching, and I speak about them when I'm invited to address various organizations or coaches or, frankly, whenever anyone will listen.

You don't have to be a coach to know we all are examples to each other—we teach, we learn, we grow, we change. What are people learning from you?

OUTSIDE OF MEADOR PHARMACY, DUMAS, AR

Chapter Four

ON LIVING WELL IN THE DASH

We all will die someday, but how many of us will truly live before that happens? I don't recall ever thinking about that in my teenage years, nor in my twenties or thirties. But now, at forty-nine, I'm starting to reflect and ask myself some of those tougher questions.

The asking is the easy part; the answering is what's difficult. The part that causes pain is coming to grips with the opportunities I let slip through my fingers, or recognizing honestly how I'd treated some people. I can deal with most of my mistakes, but there are a few that I still consider cringe-worthy. In fact, I thought I'd dealt with one memory in particular at an earlier age, but I guess not as it still seems to ease its way into my thoughts every now and again.

Growing up as an only child of a widowed mother proved to be difficult at times, as she spent her days mowing yards, raking leaves, and cleaning houses to make ends meet. While most of my friends had brothers or sisters to keep them company, I was left to my own devices. I soon found a release in sports: I'd play anything with a ball involved, but soon gravitated, as most young boys do, toward baseball and football. The neighbor kids and I spent our afternoons and most weekends playing in any yard, field, or court that wasn't already occupied.

Sadly, the older we got, the fewer games we played as our numbers thinned out. This trend continued into junior high and high school, as other interests like dating or jobs hijacked our attention and free time. But for me, it continued to be sports 24/7/365. If I was able to get a group together, I'd rather be playing *something*. When it came to money in our eight hundred-square-foot house on Summit Street, there wasn't much… but love and encouragement were plentiful, and for that I am grateful. I was blessed with a loving and caring mother who led by example and treated others with respect even when it wasn't returned in kind. I was taught to do the same and treat everyone equally, from CEOs to groundskeepers. I just assumed, in my naïveté, that everyone shared that same sentiment…but I learned the hard truth during the autumn of my junior year.

One of my very best friends growing up was Kara Beth Canada. Her family ran the town drug store, Meador Pharmacy, just across the railroad tracks off Main Street, and still owns it to this very day. Unlike today's superstores, Meador's was an amazing place for us kids to go on Saturday mornings. Picture an old-school pharmacy at which you could drop off your prescription and grab some toys, magazines, or household items while you waited. But by far my favorite activity involved the long bar that ran north to south along the east wall, where the soda fountain, ice cream, and made-to-order grilled ham and cheese sandwiches were housed. At that time of our lives, that was *our* place on Saturday mornings…even if we had to share it with the old-timers. Far beyond prescriptions and shampoos, it was a place where the old men gathered to drink coffee and tell lies about their fishing exploits, hunters showed off their trophies, and game wardens might drop by with an alligator to awe us. We considered ourselves lucky if we got there early enough to grab a barstool and sit at the counter; latecomers either had to stand or try and wedge themselves into booths that seemingly were constructed for kindergarteners. Either way, we felt like we owned the place from 11 am to 1 pm every Saturday.

At Meador's, our normal routine was to scour the newspaper until we found the write-up from the football game the night before and hope the coach got the stats in. We'd search frantically to see which players were mentioned by name, the number of yards gained, and other details. And during this review, several of us would gather by the soda fountain and try our luck with the tuna fish or grilled sandwiches; it was a way to fill your belly *and* get your ego stroked by the old-timers. You might even have gotten consoled after a tough loss, but that always seemed to depend on whether you'd corrected your mistakes. In any case, we had an appreciative audience.

But one day in particular, it also was the place where I learned my first real life lesson on how thoughtless some people can be. Adults say kids can be cruel, and while that's often true, it doesn't minimize how hurtful some grown-ups can be as well. That Saturday, I ran into a few of my friends' parents. Each congratulated me on the team's victory the night before and complimented me on my play in particular—how we really took it to our rivals from thirty miles down the road. Honestly, it felt great; we'd beaten one of the toughest teams on our schedule, and I'd scored. I felt accomplished and happy…but what happened next would shape how I'd view myself for the next twenty years.

Both sets of parents found a seat across the room and began to talk, but the problem was that Meador's wasn't very big at all—you could hear practically every conversation whether you wanted to or not. The next words out of their mouths were things no one should hear, much less a teenager: They said I was a bum, a loser—that I wouldn't make anything out of myself or my life.

I was devastated.

In one breath, they told me they were proud, and in the next, they assassinated my character and crushed my self-esteem. I may as well have been sitting in the booth with them; I heard it plain as day but still couldn't believe it. The hurt was palpable, and something changed in me that day. I might have understood their comments if I had been the type to make horrible decisions or terrorize those around me, but I wasn't; in fact, I was the kid who drove *their* kids around while they drank beer and sipped Boone's Farm Strawberry Hill—just so they wouldn't hurt themselves or anyone else.

And, since I was taught to respect others, especially adults, I wasn't sure how to deal with this, especially in public. I'd just been to their homes two days earlier, hanging out with their kids, and nothing seemed out of the ordinary. I was confused as well as embarrassed, and it seemed my best option was to sneak out the side door before I could learn whether anyone else had heard the same comments.

I don't believe I have graced those barstools at that soda fountain ever since.

Those unprovoked, ill-willed comments set me on a course to prove everyone wrong because, in my mind, if *they* thought that way about me, then I assumed everyone else must feel the same. But it was that type of thinking that caused me to make some of the biggest mistakes of my life.

After college, I poured everything I had into becoming successful, even though I had no idea of what true success really was. After getting married, I worked endlessly to make our business profitable and, for the most part, it was. I was on the right track, but it never seemed like it was good enough. I always thought I wanted more, but now, looking back, what I really wanted was those people in my small home town to know what I'd become. In fact, I wanted to force my "success" down their throats so far that no soda fountain beverage could wash it out. Instead, we ventured into real estate and other opportunities but neglected the very business that had brought what I deemed success. Without getting into too many painful details, let's just say our downfall was neither pretty nor graceful. It was humbling, and rightfully so: My family suffered because of my hubris. But I learned a valuable life lesson during this long and painful process, and I now use it as a teaching tool for my players today: **Do things for the right reason**.

You see, my motives for "success" were all wrong. They had nothing to do with honoring God and all He had done for me and my family, but rather were about proving others wrong. I believe my intentions made it so God was not comfortable blessing my endeavors. I understand that now, but way back then, I didn't really know who I was, much less *Whose* I was. Now, I tell my athletes they are the kids of a King, and they are flawless in His eyes. I try to relay to them what I wish a coach or a mentor had taught me in my impressionable years: If you want to improve, work to get better for your teammates and yourself. Set the right example. Strive to improve so you can honor God first and be good stewards of the talents given to you specifically.

Years ago, our girls' team was playing at a tournament in Bixby,

Oklahoma, and they just couldn't figure how to get over the hump. By this time, they'd actually learned how to compete and get ahead, but the problem was they hadn't figured out how to close out the games. Plain and simple, they didn't know how to win. They'd developed their skill set to the point where they could get the lead, but they just didn't have the confidence to keep it. I believe learning how to win is a process. First, you learn how to compete. Second, you learn how to not get blown out and to keep the scores close. Third, you learn how to take (and then keep) the lead. Then, after you've learned all this and won a few games, you start to believe you will win even before you lace up your cleats. This feeling allows you to take the field with a certain swagger, a confidence, and while you may not win every time you grace the field, you *expect* to, and that expectation changes your mindset. When this happens, you'll change the culture to one of expectation, discipline, accountability and, above all, winning.

We were somewhere in between steps two and three in this process, toggling back and forth. The kids and their parents were frustrated in addition to the coaches. We had dropped two more close games, both in the last inning. To add insult to injury, opponents and classmates were making our girls feel second rate, unknowingly planting seeds of doubt in their fertile minds, and their self-esteem was taking a hit. We could start to see anger rising up almost equal to our frustration.

The questions raced through our minds, players and coaches alike: *Were we really improving? Am I with the right organization? Do we as coaches know what we're talking about? Is this even worth it? If we are as close of teammates as our coaches tell us we are, why haven't we won at least one game?* Everyone wanted to win, especially the players. They were at the point to where they wanted to win simply to rub it in the faces of their doubters.

Sound familiar?

I was struggling as to how to handle this. While trying to collect my thoughts on the ride between the field and the hotel, I felt a very familiar feeling arise, like I'd been down this road before. How could I help them to not make the same mistake I made that took me twenty-plus years to overcome?

It finally came to me. *The Dash:* I would have them define their dash.

In a closed-door meeting with players and parents, we asked several questions:

1. Why are you here?
2. What do you want to accomplish?
3. How do you want to be remembered?
4. How many lives do you want to touch?
5. When others mention you, what do you want them to say?

Everyone soon figured out this wasn't about softball or closing out games at all. It was about affecting others in a positive way and leaving a legacy. It was about winning, alright, but it was about winning at *life*. I asked players to take some time and write their own eulogies, knowing full well this request could be viewed, at best, as rather morbid or downright weird. (This was confirmed by the confused looks on most faces, but here are some highlights.)

Taylor lived her life unafraid of failure. Just knowing that changed her life for the better… She gave 100% of herself to everything and everyone she came in contact with because she knew that anything else would be a slight.

Lexington taught me to be strong-willed but compassionate, practical but ambitious, and above all, to love others… God was so present in her life. She always put God first and raised her family in a godly environment… She is the strongest woman I know and I will always look up to her. She was and always will be my hero.

Hannah is remembered as a goofy, shy and trustworthy leader and business owner; a wonderful wife, mother and daughter; and a Christ follower. She put God and family first in everything she did. Most of her life was driven to help other people.

After this exercise, I explained that softball really is just a very small chapter in the book that is our life. Holding a volume from my briefcase and turning from one chapter to the next, I began to explain my thought process.

We can pinpoint our first (birth) and final (death) chapters in our books of life, but we need to focus more on the chapters in between. Driving this point home a little harder, I had them focus on a picture of a headstone. As they gazed, I began to explain the significance of the "dash" between the date of birth and the date of death…*because this is where* **life** *happens.*

If you've ever visited a cemetery, then you probably have noticed that most all headstones have a few things in common: the name of the deceased, the date of birth, the date of death and maybe a quote or a Scripture. Most people overlook the dash in between but, to me, that's the most significant part. It's where life is lived, mistakes are made, sins are forgiven, children are born, relationships are formed, loved ones are mourned, losses occur, songs are sung, and love is found. It's where plenty of questions get asked, but only some get answered. In the dash, we get to choose how we will be remembered and how many people we affect in a positive way. Simply put, the dash captures why we're here.

I could tell it started to sink in; the bewildered looks soon turned to head nods and smiles. They were finally getting it.

We all have a story to tell or a book to write. The magnificent thing is that we hold the pen, and our life's experiences are our paper. We get to determine what is written on each page of every chapter in our very own book of life. And we can choose to fill our dashes by having a positive impact on others' lives or we can choose to tear them down.

I remind my two kids, Hannah and Hayden, that they are "elevators": They're either bringing people up or taking them down. My advice to them is to always push the button that takes you and everyone with you to the penthouse. Don't settle for the basement.

Softball and baseball are just games, nothing more. If you can look past the game and focus on the metaphors below the surface, consider yourself fortunate. And if you are lucky enough to have a coach who understands, and players who "get it," then you have formed a real team and will develop a group of players who will succeed in every aspect of their lives.

Success in life can be defined in many ways. To me, it's no longer about money or possessions as it was when I was younger. Today, it's more about being content with how my life has turned out—about impacting families and spreading the Good News.

It's all about the dash.

GIRLS GOOFING OFF IN BETWEEN GAMES, STARKVILLE, MS

Chapter Five

ON DEFINING A LEADER

How do you define a leader? To the average person, it might seem pretty cut and dried but, in reality, it's not. Some might assume the most vocal player on the field or in the dugout is the leader by default, but that isn't always the case. Over the years, I have come in contact with several different types of leaders. Some are very vocal and tend to speak their thoughts out loud all the time, kind of like an old school coach on the field. They help to get the players positioned properly and keep everyone tuned in. They recall and relay the batters' approach during their last at bat, and that helps keep everyone on their toes. Next, you have your "cheerleaders": These folks are always upbeat and vital to the morale of the team. They work hard to keep the players excited on the field and in the dugout. Then you have your "strong and silents": They lead mostly by example. They seem to speak only when they have something meaningful to say. Teammates tend to listen intently when these quiet leaders speak because, more often than not, their play on the field usually speaks volumes. The players know when this type of leader opens his or her mouth, it doesn't happen very often…so you'd better pay close attention.

Some athletes exude leadership from day one; with others, it's learned over time. Lance and I decided to take our NWA Legends 99 travel team down to a camp at Mississippi State University that was hosted by the Bulldogs coaching staff. The nearly week-long camp consisted of two games daily along with instructional breakout sessions throughout each day and into the evenings. The parents were left back home; it was just us coaches and our spouses and our players. We asked that each player take full advantage of every opportunity that was offered, and they did not disappoint.

The camp was amazing, and we all took some great lessons home with us that have helped in the years since. After loading the fifteen-passenger van with gear, suitcases and each other, we headed for home. In and around the usual jokes, laughter, pranks, and quizzes about who was dating whom, the conversation turned to leadership. We pitched questions about traits, and attitudes, and eventually asked the kids to think about leaving a legacy. These are the questions I love, and I was all too happy to share my thoughts. As we touched on several topics, I realized the importance of some common denominators and the impact individuals can make.

When it comes to leaders and leadership (one of my favorite topics to speak and teach on), here are some of my top rules and favorite tenets.

Trust Only Motion: I believe this is why, when a silent leader speaks up, they have everyone's attention, including coaches—*because their play on the field is their leadership*. You can already trust their "motion". If a player is a vocal leader, he'd better back it up with his play, or it will soon be apparent his are only words, falling on deaf ears. Remember this: Don't follow a man, because if you do you will always be disappointed. Follow his *principles*.

Don't Count The Cost. Always Check The Value: There are no real statistics when it comes to success. Everyone who chooses to makes it; you need only to have a sense of urgency to be successful. Dreams determine your destiny, but discipline determines whether you will reach your goals in life. This means prioritizing your time, refusing to be a victim of failure, and rising up after you've been knocked down. It is that simple…although simple is not always easy. You must set your mind to that channel, and then break off the knob.

Be Consistent: For this, I mean *embrace the grind*. Life is full of ups and downs, but unfortunately most people learn more from the downs. (Those seem to be life's greatest teachers sometimes.) The trick is to be consistent regardless of whether you are experiencing blessings or setbacks, whether you are energized or depleted. Leaders set goals and follow through, and all breakthroughs begin with a change in beliefs.

Learn From The Past: It's up to you to decide when you are going to stop letting the past control your future. It's been said there's no distance on this Earth as far away as yesterday. Your past is just that—your *past*. No matter how hard you try, you can't change it… but you *can* learn from it. Think about the following: *Never insert a question mark where God has placed a period* and *In vehicles, there is a reason that the windshield is larger than the rearview mirror.* There is so much more waiting for you *ahead*, so carry what you've learned…but don't dwell on yesterday.

Don't Wait On Success: True leaders keep on moving, knowing they can create success instead of sitting on the sidelines. Remember: Success won't lower its standards to meet us…so we must continually raise our standards to meet it. If you get the results you seek every time, then that means your standards are way too low. Equality is not necessarily the goal when it comes to success: The extra work and time you put in gives you the right to be unequal. Leaders understand that you aren't remembered by how you start, but rather by how you finish. (In fact, our team epitomized that statement, starting at 0-19 our first year and ending as World Series runners-up our second.)

Be Thankful: Strong leaders know that negative thinking will always lead to failure and nervousness, but positive thinking will lead to a happy, healthy, abundant life. We will always be thankful for the things we choose to see. If all you see is negative, then you will never be thankful for the things you don't see. Don't be a person who is waiting on others to bless them, but rather be a person who's a blessing to others. Being thankful makes you more productive, and saying "thank you" is an act of leadership. Luke 17:11-19 describes how Jesus healed ten lepers, but only one came back to thank Him. It wasn't that the others weren't thankful—I'm sure they were—but they simply didn't take the time to say so. Learn to have an attitude of gratitude.

Develop Mental Toughness: Being an optimist after you've already gotten everything doesn't count. People are looking for ways to perform for others, starving for Camelot—that notion of a special group of people who support one another and are devoted to a particular cause. They have a thirst for what leaders possess, and want to believe in a team (and want a team to believe in them in return). The more challenges a leader faces, the more dynamic the leader will become. The sign of a champion is not what one says or does when things are going well, but rather how one handles the circumstances that come when life isn't perfect. Here is a prime example: Two men are fishing far out in the middle of the ocean, and the great Moby Dick breaches the water's surface between their two boats. One man moans and screams, "Why me?"; the other man rejoices and yells, "Where's the tartar sauce and hush puppies?" It's all about perspective and attitude. Mental toughness means seeking out the pressure that can't be avoided and becoming energized by it.

Understand How You See The Problem *Is* The Problem: Leaders know the opposite of success is not failure, it's quitting. They know success is built upon failure after failure. Leaders also know the function of leadership is to produce more *leaders*, not more followers, and they know you can't judge *and* love others at the same time. I once read a great and thought-provoking question: *If you received ten cents for every kind word you spoke and five cents for every unkind word, would*

32

you be rich or poor? Be a river of good words, not a dam, and learn to view problems as opportunities.

Be Committed: Leaders display dedication to a cause or a team. They have an expectation of excellence…and excellence is never an accident. They exceed expectations by doing the right thing, with deep roots in integrity, and honesty, and fairness. They believe in teamwork and that striving together toward a common vision fuels ordinary people to achieve amazing things. Leaders set the pace and stay a step ahead of others and, for the most part, are risk-takers: They're willing to part with security to pursue the unknown. They are consistent and persistent, trying, stumbling, and adjusting because they are comfortable with facing failure regularly. Leaders don't concern themselves with others' opinions; they understand when you give the right of approval to someone else, you also give them the right to control your dreams. If your standards are low, you will accept anyone on your team as a player or a doer, but leaders won't accept anyone who's not ready to perform at a certain level. They may embrace everyone as a teammate, but they also know there's a difference between being a teammate and a "doer"…and they are committed to motivating doers into action.

Leave Legacies: Leaders know how they want to live, their abilities and opportunities, and the messages they want to leave behind. You don't get to choose how or when you are going to die, but you *can* choose how you want to live. We are free to choose our actions, but we are not free to choose the consequences of our actions. You can live your life any way you want, but you only get to live it once. Pour into those God has placed in your path so when you aren't around, they'll still believe in themselves. Be on the lookout for their strengths and bring those to the forefront. Believe in others and teach them to teach others.

This is how leaders change the world: one choice, one action, one kind word at a time.

On that ride home from camp, day soon yielded to night and boisterous chatter gave way to blessed silence, allowing me and Lance to reminisce about how far our players had come as a team. The evidence was plain to see on the field: They had won six of the first seven tournaments they'd entered…not to mention they'd lost that championship game at the Mississippi State tournament by only one run, with two outs in the last inning. Their play and their confidence obviously had improved by leaps and bounds. But honestly, I was more concerned with how they were progressing outside of softball. We questioned just how much each player retained when it came to the mental aspect of the game and our talks; retaining and retrieving takes practice and initiative, and we knew this was as important (if not more) than simply building skills. So as we pulled into the parking lot back home, each player was challenged to find ways to lead and to show leadership. We challenged them to practice these new-found traits in their homes, classrooms, churches and, of course, on the field.

I've found that most teams consist of several types of personalities, the combination of which builds the whole team simply by dynamics. I liken it to cooking: If you want to make a great batch of jambalaya, you must use more than just one or two flavors. It takes many different ingredients in the right amounts to make it not just palatable, but truly delicious. But let me tell you one thing I've learned: Once you mix those ingredients in the perfect proportions, it's as close to Heaven as this ol' boy can imagine.

As time went on, travel ball gave way to high school ball, and we were anxious to see just how much knowledge each player retained and applied to their everyday life. I've made it a point to see at least one high school game for each athlete I've coached, and what I've witnessed is nothing short of amazing. I've seen our quiet young ladies become more at ease outside of their comfort zones, leading well on the field, in the dugout, and in the coach's huddle. I've watched them lift each other's spirits and heard them actually recite a few highlights from our talks. On two separate occasions, I've observed our players take over the huddle and reassure her teammates, which was instrumental in building belief for their eventual comebacks.

And this priceless growth and maturity took place *after* their coaches had all but given up.

I can leave those games now with a feeling of accomplishment, knowing we made a difference. It's the very best a leader can hope for.

As I wind down this chapter, let me pose a question: What type of leader are you? All are important but, in my opinion, there is something special and significant about being a servant leader. Do you serve others, or are you self-serving? I've learned that being willing to serve in the smallest of ways reveals the biggest rewards. Such a willingness to help indicates our hearts are open to discover other ways to serve. Jesus of course is the best model of servant leadership, with examples throughout the Bible. When John 13:1-17 talks about Jesus washing the disciples' feet, we see the servant leader paradox in full force: "Very truly I tell you, no servant is greater than his master, nor is a messenger greater than the one who sent him" (John 13:16, NIV).

Our organization was blessed to have a fantastic example of a servant leader in Coach Jerry Kelton. He was always the first to volunteer. It didn't matter how trivial the task; if he overheard a coach, parent, or player mention they needed something or had lost something, he was off to either fix it or find it, almost always without being asked. From him, I soon realized that coaching these kids was a form of serving. It had never dawned on me until then.

I realized that to teach anything, I first had to learn, so I grew myself, by default. I felt I had to make sure I was ready with the right things to say and do at any given time, and for me to do that, I needed to spend extra time researching and reading. This had a profound effect on how I approached my wife, my kids, my friends, and my job: By serving others, *every aspect of my life improved.* That was not my intention, but I welcomed it like a crawfish pie greets a steaming pan of jalapeno cornbread. *Delish!*

A true leader humbly tends to others, and receives blessings far greater than he or she bestows. *Give before you are asked and serve others; the ones who serve the most will be leaders of all.* It starts with us: We show up to serve and start to like ourselves, and that liking ourselves teaches us to love others. There is no better play for true happiness.

COACH KEITH AND JADYN AFTER THEIR LAST GAME WAS OVER

Chapter Six

ON CHOOSING TO ENCOURAGE

When it comes down to it, sporting contests are just games and nothing more. I try to emphasize this to my kids and my players, because in the moment it's easy to elevate them to a place they shouldn't be. Instead, I ask these kids (and try, myself) to find regular opportunities to lift up others, because you never know what they may be going through at any given time.

This tenet became painfully clear during one of our recent tournaments. Our team had finished a game and wasn't scheduled to play again for two hours. There wasn't enough time to go to the hotel, so we decided to hang around and watch a few other teams play. We settled in to watch the group we were scheduled to play later that evening. The game was nip and tuck until the fifth inning, when one player made a mistake that led to a few runs and, subsequently, her team's loss.

We then watched in horror as the coach berated this fourteen-year-old as though she'd committed a felony. Our team, unknowingly, just happened to be sitting near her parents during this fiasco. As wrenching as it was for us, I could only imagine how it felt for the parents, let alone the player. It was, in a word, unconscionable. We gathered our team and headed for the pavilion, all the while feeling heartbroken about what we had just witnessed.

Later that evening, we happened to run into the same player and her family in the parking lot, and we expressed our dismay over how she was treated. A couple of our players made sure to point out some of the great plays she had, and how the score wouldn't have even been that close had it not been for her stellar hitting. Not knowing if our girls' words carried any weight to her hurting heart, we parted ways and started toward a restaurant before the long ride home. A few minutes later as we were leaving, our paths crossed again. We exchanged few cordial waves and pleasantries as we opened the doors to our vehicle and they walked toward the restaurant. As we were backing out of the space, readying for the two-hour drive, her father tapped on the window and asked me to thank our girls for the kind words they had spoken to his daughter. He explained that she had been experiencing some rough times lately with the loss of a very close family member, and how she really enjoyed softball because it gave her an escape from reality for a few short hours. The events that took place earlier in the day had her questioning her love for the sport but, after talking with our girls, she was willing to continue playing the game she loved.

That interaction was such an affirmation to what we were teaching our players. It also impressed on our kids that they can indeed make a difference. As the miles passed by, the conversation was free-flowing. We spoke about how some people don't have encouragers in their lives and how we should be open for God to use us as He sees fit. Our girls saw the beauty in being a blessing to others, and here are a few of the ways they discovered they could do so.

Look for ways to build belief in others: Find individuals' good points and accentuate those. Don't focus on weaknesses or flaws; rather, pick out their strengths and emphasize each one individually. People already have plenty of others tearing them down and telling them they can't do any number of things. *Be the person who lets them know they can.* God's Word says "He is no respecter of persons"—in other words, in His eyes, no one is better or worse than another. God doesn't play favorites, but rather gives generously to all who ask and seek Him.

Compliment quickly and frequently: Let others know you care for them along with sharing all the good they've done in your life.

Have your words describe how they've made a difference for you. It may be the only good thing they hear that day, week, month, or even year. It doesn't matter how successful someone looks on the outside; chaos could be growing wild on the inside…and all they need is a few kind words to keep the darkness at bay. In God's eyes, our pasts have been forgiven; we don't need to dwell on the things we've done wrong. Encouragement is like watering a dry plant; it quenches our thirst and gives us hope for a new day, reassuring us that we're remarkable, valuable and unique.

Focus on positive words: I've talked about being an elevator and either bringing others up or taking them down with our words and actions. We asked our players: *What kind of person do you want to be? How do you want others to speak of you?* Be the one to breathe life into others, not take life from them. Jeremiah 29:11 reads, "For I know the plans I have for you," declares the Lord, "plans to prosper you and not to harm you, plans to give you hope and a future" (NIV). God's plan for your life is for you to be prosperous, not lacking in the things that really matter. He wants us to enjoy life, not to dread the future. We can be the example others point to (and the ones they turn to) when they are in need.

Here's an example that hits a little closer to home…from one of the lowest points in my life. When people say things like, "This just isn't my day," any normal person can relate because we all have had times when things just don't fall into place, no matter how we try. I knew that feeling oh-so-well, actually, because my family was having a "This just hasn't been our twelve- to fifteen months" kind of thing. My business wasn't doing well, our income was only one-third of normal, and I had to pick and choose which bills I could pay while putting others on hold, falling further behind. My kids didn't seem to want to do things with me like they had when they were younger, like going to the ballfield, and activities that used to be considered fun (like hitting or taking infield) seemed to be a bother for them. They had reached those ages when they'd rather have worked with another player's parent or a different coach…or even have stayed home altogether. My relationship with my wife wasn't where it needed to be after twenty years of marriage. I owed the IRS $30,000. My daughter was heading off to college to play softball, and I couldn't figure out how I was going to pay for it.

I just couldn't seem to get caught up, much less ahead. Maybe you can relate?

Frankly, I didn't enjoy my job anymore and found myself stressed and spiraling more and more into darkness. And the thoughts running rampant through my head were turning darker, too, and just piling it on: *Why are you even here? No one would miss you if you were gone. You aren't making a difference in anyone's life, anyway. You don't have any friends who are there for you. It is funny how, if they need a kind word or advice when things aren't going right, they don't hesitate to call you, but when you need the same, they make you feel like you are a nuisance…*

There was a battle going on like in the old cartoons, with an angel on my right shoulder and the devil on the left, each arguing as if we were in a court of law. To be honest, the guy on the left—spewing all kinds of venom—was winning. It even got to the point where he helpfully reminded me I had over a million dollars in life insurance and my wife and kids might be better off without me. I kept asking the guy on the right for help and to plead his case for my reason to keep living. I begged him to let me know whether I was making a difference in anyone's life.

No response. *Nothing.*

During those dark days, the only thing keeping my mind out of that mental war was being in between the lines of a ball field. You see, when I invest in my athletes or spend time on the field, my whole outlook changes. I forget my worries, stress isn't an issue, and relationship challenges aren't weighing down my thoughts. I am just on the field helping people, which, in turn, helps me.

One Sunday afternoon I decided to get in my truck and take a drive to contemplate the future: *Where do I go from here?* Leaving the driveway, I stopped by the box to get yesterday's mail. Honestly, I rarely check it; Dana or the kids normally do that but, for some reason, I felt compelled that day. There were a few things left over from Saturday's mail run—a financial aid packet from Hannah's college, a bill or two, and an envelope addressed to me. It had a familiar return address but no name. Sitting at the mailbox with my truck still running, I opened it and began to read.

It was quite possibly the nicest, kindest letter I'd ever received from a player I'd coached, letting me know what a difference I'd made in her life. She said how much she appreciated that I was a servant leader, an encourager, and an "uplifter" of others. It was, simply, a thank you letter—genuine and heartfelt, a simple gesture from a seventeen-year-old ballplayer to her forty-nine-year-old coach.

But, oh—what a difference it made in this man's life! That one-page handwritten letter helped me realize I really do make a difference, that I have a unique purpose. Sometimes the coach needs to be reminded of what he tells his players—that God doesn't make junk. His Word says He knew us before we were born, and that He has a plan for our lives. When we surrender to His will, not our own, we'll begin to live in our purpose…our sweet spot.

My centerfielder thought she was thanking me for making a difference in her life, but she had no clue about the significant difference she'd just made in her coach's life—the type of difference that matters, that makes facing tomorrow bearable, that gives hope to the hopeless and joy to the joyless. We know that with just one small sliver of hope, a person can become unstoppable, unbreakable, and unbelievably strong.

God uses different people to speak to us. While I was hurting, I wanted and expected my wife, my kids, my closest friends and even my pastor to speak encouragement into my life. But God commissioned one of the least expected people to brighten my day and give me strength. He asked; she answered. When we think we have it all figured out, God has His own way of letting us know that He is still in charge and on the throne.

He is a God of paradoxes. He sent Moses, who had a stuttering problem and lacked confidence, to tell the King of Egypt to let God's people go so he could lead the Israelites to the Promised Land. In 2

Kings 4, God sent Elisha to help a widow whose husband had died and whose two sons were about to be taken as slaves by providing an overflowing oil supply. And he sent a quiet, reserved centerfielder to reassure her coach at the time it was needed most.

The truth is, He knows who needs to hear from you, and when. Even right now, odds are that someone in your circle needs some hope in a desperate way—a hope that you can provide. We become encouragers by emulating our Great Encourager: Are you willing to answer His call?

LEGENDS 99 TEAM BANNER

Dear Coach Keith,

I am writing to you today because Coach Harper challenged us to find servant leaders in our lives. When he defined a servant leader as selfless, willing to drop everything to help another out, I immediately thought of you.

So today, I just want to thank you. Thank you for always keeping my spirits up even when I'm down, especially in the batter's box. Thank you for the endless amounts of rides you have given me so that I have the opportunity to play the sport I love. Thank you for investing so much of your time so that I and everyone else can further our career as a softball player. Thank you for getting mad at us when we suck, and laughing with us when we are kicking butt.

I look up to you in so many ways, especially as a leader. When I started playing for you, I would have never said a word, but your constant encouragement helped me to get out of my shell, and try my best to be a good example to my teammates.

I want to conclude by saying, I don't know what my plans are for the future, but I know that whatever I choose, whether it be softball or not, you will have my back and I know if I ever need a little heart to heart or anything, I will always have someone to call. So, once again, I thank you for all you have done. Thank you for being a great servant leader in my life.

Yours Truly,
Jadyn Heinle

TEAM PICTURE IN ANKENY, IA

HANNAH HURST SIGNING DAY WITH HAYDEN, MOM, AND DAD

TWO TOURNAMENT WINS

HANNAH & HAYDEN IN THE GOOD OLD DAYS

LEGENDS 99 TEAM WATCHING THE MOVIE "WHEN THE GAME STANDS TALL"

LEGENDS 99 2ND PLACE WIN IN CABOT, AR

TAYLOR HULL SIGNING DAY

SOFTBALL TEAM BANNER

COACHING LITTLE LEAGUE IN DUMAS, AR

HAYDEN AND HIS TEAMMATES HIS SOPHOMORE YEAR BEFORE A GAME

LEGENDS 99 AND THE LEGENDS 08 TOGETHER AT A TOURNAMENT

RECOGNIZING THE COMMITTED PLAYERS WITH A GIFT

LEGENDS 99 SERVING AT THE SAMARITAN HOUSE

ALYSSA "AJ" DOWNEY SIGNING DAY

HAYDEN HURST WITH HIS AUNTIE LISA

BOOTHS INSIDE MEADOR PHARMACY IN DUMAS, AR

TEAM DADS' PHEASANT HUNT

HANNAH HURST SIGNING DAY

LEGENDS 99 ENJOYING ICE CREAM IN STARKVILLE, MS

END OF THE YEAR CHRISTMAS AWARDS BANQUET AND DINNER

HANNAH, JADYN AND TAYLOR GETTING THAT LAST PICTURE IN TOGETHER

LEGENDS ORGANIZATION BANQUET RECOGNIZING THE TEAM THAT STARTED IT

SOFTBALL GIRLS AFTER PLACING IN A TOURNAMENT

LEGENDS 99 TAKING A BREAK FROM TRAVELING AT A ROADSIDE PARK
ON THEIR WAY TO MISSISSIPPI STATE

HAYDEN & HANNAH'S USUAL PIC AFTER EACH FOOTBALL GAME

LEXINGTON DOBBS SIGNING DAY

TEAM'S 1ST TOURNAMENT WIN IN MONET, MO

TEAM SELFIE AFTER TAKING 2ND PLACE IN CABOT, AR

BROOKE BOSTON SIGNING DAY

SODA FOUNTAIN INSIDE MEADOR PHARMACY

LEGENDS 99'S VERY LAST GAME IN KANSAS CITY, MO

HANNAH & HAYDEN: GROWING UP ON THE FIELD, FALL 2010

HAYDEN AT CENTER

Chapter Seven

ON BEING PREPARED

How deep is the mud? Well, it depends on whether you ask a giraffe or an ant. We all go through the same stuff differently. Life is like an onion: You peel it back one layer at a time…and sometimes you cry. But just because you've feared and stumbled and fallen doesn't mean anything. The last chapter of your book hasn't been written yet, and if people judge you now, they will have judged you prematurely. Someone's opinion of you, especially where fear is concerned, doesn't have to become your reality…especially if you've worked on being prepared.

Elkins High School football practice usually runs long on Tuesdays. It's the day of the week when coaches install their offensive game plan and develop their defensive schemes. I call it "implementation day"—a long work day for both boys and coaches. It's also the day I swing by after work and pick up my son, Hayden. I try to get there early enough to catch the tail end of practice if possible. As Hayden climbed into the truck this particular Tuesday, we exchanged our usual "How was practice?" inquiry and "Good!" reply.

As with most teenagers, it's very difficult to carry on a meaningful conversation when their replies consist mostly of one-word answers. Dana and I have learned over time to ask more probing and open-ended questions with the hope of tricking our two kids into having an actual dialog. That Tuesday, however, was quite different. The conversation was unusually one-sided, flowing from him to me for a change (and thankfully I've also learned to keep quiet when our kids get on a roll and just enjoy the process).

He said the team's defense for the next Friday night game had a nose guard. This was a topic of interest because he plays center…and the nose guard scheduled to be directly across the line from him happened to be six-foot-seven and nearly four hundred pounds. At first, I thought he must be exaggerating—*that big, in high school? No way*—he had to be *mistaken.* Hayden is five-foot-ten and maybe one seventy-five on a good day. I asked how he felt about going up against a guy that doubled his weight and had him by nine inches in height. *Wasn't he concerned?* (Truth be told, I also was remembering the old joke about a captain of a vessel floating at sea who saw a pirate ship quickly approaching. He told one of his mates to run and get his red shirt because, if he got shot, he didn't want the enemy or his crew to see him bleed. As the man took off to get the red shirt, the captain looked again and saw ten more pirate ships floating alongside the first. He yelled back to his mate, "While you're down there, grab my brown pants!") But again, a stellar attitude prevailed. Hayden replied, "No, not really…but everyone else said they were glad it was me and not them!" He seemed to be energized by the challenge; in fact, I think he viewed it as an opportunity to prove his worth to the team as well as the coaching staff.

As the conversation continued, we talked about faith verses fear and how people allow the latter to run (and ruin) their lives. I believe we have the option to allow fear to enter and rule our lives, or not. And if we do, it means we believe more in what Satan can do than what God can do. Like oil and water, faith and fear don't mix well. Fear will contaminate your faith and put handcuffs on God in an attempt to hobble what He can do.

Hayden realized he needed to trust his coaching and his training. He happened to be one of only a couple of sophomores who garnered playing time, much less a starting position on a team full of talented seniors. He earned his position fair and square during summer practices and two-a-days. But this would prove to be his toughest test yet, in more ways than one. He went into his room every night after dinner to study film on his upcoming opponent, hoping to find a few weaknesses or tendencies he might be able to exploit during the game. He wanted to gain an advantage in the proper way.

We talked a lot during the week leading up to the game—about how we can be motivated but not have momentum, and how we won't get far unless those two things worked together. It's our responsibility to come up with the vision, but vision will only be propelled to completion through motivation and momentum. We also talked about getting beyond believing, when that means we're only trying to convince ourselves of something. The harder part is getting to *knowing*, to a true faith. Faith that doesn't have "legs" won't get us anywhere.

Luke 8:43-48 tells about a woman who bled for over twelve years. She heard Jesus was close and believed she could be healed if she could just get close enough to Him. As Jesus walked, He was surrounded by all kinds of people who were tugging at and brushing up against him. Since she wasn't able to get close enough to speak with him, she relied on her faith—reaching out and touching his robe instead. Instantly, she was healed...but then Jesus stopped and asked who'd touched Him as He'd felt His energy leave. When she confessed what she had done, the woman heard the words she longed for: "Daughter, your faith has healed you. Go in peace" (NIV).

The touch of faith: Imagine what we could accomplish if we had this type of faith instead of fear.

After Hayden and I spent that week readying to meet his opponent, Dana and I entered the stadium...and it wasn't hard to locate the enormous man-child our son would be facing. While we waited for the opening kickoff, several parents made their way over to us as if to give us their condolences on what was surely about to happen. I have to admit, I was a little nervous myself but, against the odds, Hayden held his own for the most part. A few parents called it a modern day David-and-Goliath story, but this time the outcome was different: Our boys lost by a touchdown. Some untimely penalties, a few high snaps down by the goal line, and blown coverages led to the defeat.

Hayden was crushed. He was not the reason they lost, but he contributed his fair share of missteps. He felt he'd let his team down by not trusting his preparation and getting anxious on a few plays.

67

The ride home was rather quiet, and we didn't talk much about the game until around noon the next day. Hayden knew we were proud of him and his effort. He faced a tough task and, for the most part, did his job well. While losses can take most people some time to get over, Hayden is a little different: He watches film, acknowledges his mistakes, works at correcting them, and moves on. He knows no matter how hard he tries, he cannot change the past…so why dwell on it? He learns and continues forward. I love that about him and wish I could be more like him in that respect.

He wasn't afraid of his opposition; he hit him head-on and never flinched. It's all in how you look at it: Even a kite rises and falls against its opposition, the wind. Hayden *had* prepared: When we'd talked earlier that week about David and lessons we could learn from those Bible stories—things like preparing to make things happen instead of waiting on that big break—Hayden was already on it, mirroring a young David. You see, without even knowing it, David had prepared for his challenges as a young shepherd: He learned how to guard against threats and protect animals in his care, and already knew that some things were worth fighting for. This preparation paid off when it came his time to meet Goliath. As David prepared for that ultimate fight, King Saul and others reminded him that he was just a boy. But David countered by arguing that when a lion or a bear tried to take off with the king's sheep, he was the one to rescue the sheep *and* kill the predator. He boldly proclaimed that he would take care of the man who defied the armies of the living God. In essence, what David did was reaffirm his past successes to prepare his mind for his upcoming battle. He was ready…and when everyone else said Goliath was too big to fight, David said he was too big to miss!

As I tell my players, throughout life you will have doubters and naysayers—folks who tell you that you *can't*. When this comes from people in your own family, it's especially hard…but remind them God says you have exactly what it takes, and that's all you need to know. It's so easy for people who haven't done things to tell you you're not capable. God says you are.

Part of why I am so proud of Hayden is that he's got the heart and willingness to prepare for whatever may come. He knows he must be willing to sacrifice what he is right now for what he is becoming. There is an old Chinese proverb that states, "A man who rolls up his sleeves seldom loses his shirt." Meaning, dreams take work, so we must be prepared: You have but a short opportunity to turn your dreams into realities. And I believe if you want God to change your circumstances, you must first change your heart.

In Matthew 24:42-43, we're told to be on the alert because we don't know on which day the Lord is coming. The truth is, "Always be prepared" shouldn't just be for Boy Scouts, but for *anyone* who wants to succeed in faith and life. And after you've spent the time and effort to prepare, you then have to trust and have faith in your abilities, no matter the odds. Sometimes it's hard when things aren't going your way, but that is the exact definition of faith: Knowing that God has your back, and He has your best interests in mind, even when you can't see it.

I encourage you to have faith that God is working behind the scenes, and things are happening for a reason. Faith and trust are just like muscles; if they are not exercised on a daily basis, they'll become weak. The more you exercise your faith muscles, the easier it will be to overcome any struggle that comes. God isn't looking for perfect people; He is looking for obedient people. He desires a relationship and wants it daily.

Ordinary ballplayers can become extraordinary when they allow God to move in their lives, but we also have to be prepared to hear Him and do the next right thing. When Samson defeated the Philistines with the jawbone of a donkey, he learned the jawbone was not special; on the contrary, it was ordinary…but when God breathed His life on it, the jawbone became extraordinary. You don't have to be the most talented at anything in life, including sports; you can be average (or even below average), but when you honor God with your life, you also can become extraordinary.

All God wants us to do is to be prepared to work with what we have and let Him take care of the rest. Simply being prepared allows a great God to do great things through you.

HAYDEN HURST & FAMILY AFTER A GAME

Chapter Eight
ON LIVING IN YOUR SWEET SPOT

Science never has been nor will be my best subject. As a matter of fact, I loathed any form of it: From chemistry to biology to physics, each one was as evil as the next in my opinion. I didn't discriminate. I hated them equally. I only took the classes because my college counselor told me I had to. If not for that, I never would have darkened the doors of the Science Building at UAM.

My lone good science experience happened my freshman year when the science professor held up an Easton baseball bat, pointed to the fat part, and asked, "What is this called?" I instinctively yelled, "The sweet spot!" He laughed and said, "You're right," even though he was looking for a more scientific answer.

He was obviously a baseball fan because that's all we talked about before and after class from that day forward. I will forever be convinced the only reason I passed his class was our mutual love of the Chicago Cubs, along with our enduring appreciation for long-suffering Cubs fans. We shared a common disappointment that rolled around every September, when playoffs would start and all of Wrigley Field would be empty other than the ivy on the outfield walls.

The sweet spot. It's that area where the bat meets the ball and magical things happen. Balls fly further and with more accuracy. The handle doesn't vibrate. The sound is distinct. Everything comes together for that one moment in time, and it all just falls into place. I have often wondered how that translates into life: How many of us are living in our sweet spot? Let's take it a step further: How many of us are living life on purpose?

I asked our players to consider this very question in Oklahoma City, after a hard-fought loss dropped our team into the bottom half of the tournament (otherwise known as the "loser's bracket"). When a team finds itself down there, they must play several games, seemingly back to back to back with very little downtime, for any chance of winning the tournament. Our players had won six of their last seven tournaments leading up to Oklahoma City and seemed to be in their groove…but entering the game on that Friday night, they just looked and played out of sync. They couldn't seem to find their sweet spot.

If I were to take a poll, I would venture to say the results would show that most of us aren't living in sync…and that is a shame. I believe there's a direct correlation between living life on purpose and living in your purpose. It can be said that, in life, you're either on your way, or in the way. When I am coaching, I am on my way; when I'm not, I'm in the way. I've found that truly living in our sweet spots boils down to a few things: growth, knowledge, and implementation.

Growth: What are you doing to improve yourself? Are you reading motivating, encouraging material? I challenged our players to have three books beside their beds: one on personal growth or self-improvement, one on relationships, and (most importantly) one concerning our spirituality. We asked them to read daily to develop a habit. It's no different than taking several classes in school: Each class has a different subject matter, just like these varied books.

I believe, as humans, we're either moving forward or regressing. By making it a point to grow ourselves a little every day, we'll always be moving forward. It's similar to growing a fruit or vegetable; once they're removed from the vine or branch that gives them life, they slowly start to decay. (As an aside, if you remove yourself from the Word of God, the same could be said about your spirit!) Commit to growing yourself, and you'll find ever-increasing ways to improve.

Knowledge: I grew up in farming country down in the southeast corner of the Arkansas delta. There are three distinct seasons in farming, and they tie in very nicely to our quest for knowledge. First is *the sowing season*, when you break ground and prepare the soil to receive the seed. After the seeds have been planted, the second is *the growing season*, which is significant because it can be deceiving. It can appear that not a lot is happening; when this happens in humans, we can become complacent and discontented because we don't see any growth right away. Eventually, *the harvest season* comes…but there's plenty of scut work in between.

It's in the second season that a lot of boring tasks must be done; we've got to water the fields and weed the crops to grow top-notch produce. It's the life blood…and also the slowest and seemingly most unproductive time. But in reality, this growth season can be considered the most important of all three. The fields must be looked after carefully so they don't get taken over and choked by weeds. The same can be said about feeding and guarding our minds. We are bombarded daily with bits and pieces of negative "weeds" and if we don't take control of our thoughts, they'll take over. One way to guard your mind is by feeding it good information from books and positive affirmation talks. We need to be serious and forthright with what we allow to enter our minds.

When the harvest finally comes, it's when we get to see and take part in the culmination of what was sown—the "reward" season. It reminds me of one of my favorite verses in the Bible, Galatians 6:9: *Let us not become weary in doing good, for at the proper time we will reap a harvest if we do not give up*. When it comes to adding knowledge, we've got to keep on keeping on…especially when we don't see the growth. As long as we keep working and keep the faith, everything will come to fruition. There's an old parable about a Chinese bamboo tree, and how its growth mimics human growth. According to the story, even with the proper water, sun and nurturing, the bamboo wouldn't break ground that first year…or the next four. But the wise farmer continued to tend to it while never losing hope and, eventually, in year five, the bamboo was said to grow about eighty feet in six weeks! While this seems like a crazy amount of growth in a small window of time, isn't that what often happens to us humans, when something finally "clicks" for us? The truth is, our growing seasons, however quiet and seemingly unexciting, develop the strong and necessary root system that allows us to grow by leaps and bounds *when the time is right*. The same can be said for sculpting marble and splitting wood: It's usually not the first hit, and sometimes not even the hundredth, that finally causes the breakthrough. We must keep at it but, like the wise farmer, we must also be patient and simply keep doing the next right thing. Nothing good would have come from a farmer who pulled out a "defective" seed, lamented why it was taking so long, and berated the process; in fact, that impatience would have stunted any potential for growth. The same principle can be applied to other facets of our lives, like finances, friendships, fitness and mental/spiritual growth. I wonder how many of us have "dug up our seeds" before they were able to take root? We pray and believe for something, but if we don't get immediate results, human nature can take over, fueled by our desire for instant gratification, and, just like that, our seeds have been snatched right out of their birthplace before their time.

The growing season is surely uncomfortable, but if we stay the course, we'll always receive more in return than what we gave. These seasons of growing in knowledge also will test our faith; we shouldn't dig up our seeds because we don't see an immediate return. We have to endure the growing season—reading, weeding, adding knowledge—to reap the spoils of the harvest.

Implementation: Gaining knowledge by growing yourself means nothing unless you implement what you have learned. Use your newfound knowledge daily and release your faith, just as a farmer does when he plants seeds. When a farmer cultivates his fields, weeds the rows, and waters the soil, he is releasing his faith that the seed will not return void. And by implementing his knowledge, the farmer knows he will get more in return than what he planted.

Take corn for example: After the growing season, when it comes time to harvest his fields, the farmer sees his original, single corn seed produced a stalk, which contains several ears of corn, each of which contain hundreds of more seeds. This is a down-home example of sowing and reaping at its finest.

Another thing that can impact living in our sweet spot is complacency: When people do things for an extended period of time, they can get lax if they aren't careful. In fact, complacency seemed to have worked itself into our team that weekend in Oklahoma City. I found it confusing that our players had gotten so accustomed to winning that they just seemed to be going through the motions and possibly not giving their best effort. I mean, just a short year and a half earlier, they were struggling simply to get a win, much less become tournament champions… and here they'd won six this season.

They had unknowingly become complacent but we challenged them…and to their credit, they responded accordingly and rose to the occasion. They eventually fought their way out of the loser's bracket to place third, which was no easy feat due to the competition they faced. After some motivation and a "reset," they prepared themselves to keep on going by simply playing the way they'd practiced—full speed and no regrets.

Sometimes choosing to live in our sweet spot is more an issue of will and character. I define this as what we do or how we choose to be when no one is looking. Character is founded on unchanging principles, and it is a series of decisions we make as we grow and mature. It's not handed to us, but rather forged consistently over the years, entailing hard work and waiting. We *choose* to live life on purpose…prayerfully determining our path and moving ahead regardless of the obstacles. Develop a plan to cruise past good and move on to extraordinary. Find mentors who have accomplished what you want to do and pick their brains. Be willing to take the appropriate risks when necessary, and have knowledge that the steps you take may sometimes lead to alienation. Be prepared to take "hits" from others. Believe that God has a plan and a vision for you. Be passionate, be excited, but above all, be disciplined. Live your life with a definite purpose.

What I have found, after years of reading, teaching, learning, failing and succeeding, is that those who live life on purpose give and receive far more in life. They impact individuals and families and neighborhoods; they grow ideas and businesses; they change rules and lives. Theirs is not a quiet, invisible existence, but rather a joyous living out loud. What might happen if you ventured into your sweet spot? I believe you would feel as prosperous as Jesus indicated in Matthew 13:8…producing a crop a hundred, sixty or thirty times what was sown. Are you ready to dig in?

ANOTHER SUCCESSFUL TOURNAMENT

Chapter Nine
ON HANDLING ADVERSITY

It's been said you can't get far while you are looking in the rearview mirror, and there's a reason why your eyes are placed in the front of your head and not the back. We humans tend to use our energies reviewing our pasts rather than envisioning our futures. And while there are valuable lessons to carry along with us in life, there's far more waiting ahead of us than what we've left behind.

Toward that end, consider the following:

- Do you strive to give your best in all you do, at all times?
- Can others count on you?
- Is your word your bond?

I've found there's nothing more damaging to a person's reputation than the charge that he or she is a hypocrite. (And there's also nothing more hurtful to the one who discovers that sad truth.) Being a good and trusted leader means we give it our all to be honorable and dependable. For many of us, faith gives us the courage to live what we say and say what we live. A person who lives right and is right has more power in his or her silence than others have in all their words.

This was never more evident than in the middle of our 0-19 streak, riding home from a tournament in Tulsa. We had some tough questions to ask our kids: What did they want from this experience? What did they want to learn? More importantly...were they holding back, or giving maximum effort every time out? To our players' great credit, they answered each question strong and true, straight from the heart.

What I have found over years of working with athletes is that some have a fear of failure. Some mentally justify not giving their all because they're afraid it still might not be good enough; if that's true…then what? Others have a fear of success because they just don't trust themselves, or believe they won't be able to handle it. Either way, they sell themselves (and those around them) short and get robbed of feeling that a job was well done.

Because adversity is such a given in our lives, I often tell my players, "Give yourself a chance to do something special. Give God a chance to show up and show off." Yes, we face struggles and challenges regularly, but they often give us an opportunity to reveal our—and God's—best.

Unfortunately, adversity can impact people differently, sometimes negating the blessings it can bring. A few years back, I heard the following analogy about the effects of boiling water (adversity) on three different items: carrots, eggs, and coffee beans. Drop a hard carrot into boiling water and it will get soft—kind of like when life's pain hits and formerly strong people begin to wilt and lose their power. Now, take the egg: It starts off fragile, but becomes hard when the heat gets turned up. Some folks who seem to have softer spirits, happily loving life, become hard and rigid when faced with some "heat"—a breakup, financial difficulty, or hardship. They may look the same on the outside, but have hearts and souls of cement on the inside. Both the carrot and the egg allow the boiling water to change them, but coffee beans actually thrive in such adversity, *changing the water*—the very environment that brings the pain. When the water gets hot, coffee beans release the best they have to offer—the richest flavor, the most decadent aroma.

If you can be like coffee beans when life is at its worst, you'll find you'll get better and stronger and actually change your circumstances in the midst of adversity. When times are the hardest, you'll rise to the occasion, actually *changing your environment*.

I remember having this very conversation as we rode home from that losing tournament in Tulsa. We talked about how the happiest people don't necessarily have everything, but they make the most of everything they have. They learn to deal with whatever comes their way, including (and especially) the hard times. It's been said the brightest future will be based on a forgotten past—you can't truly move forward until you let go of your failures.

I've found these gems show up time and again in baseball and softball: These two games are the only ones in which you can fail three-quarters of the time and still be considered one of the best—even Hall of Fame-worthy. As we learn from the past and let the pain go, we find failure is just an event, not a lifestyle. When we strive to be great, we should not be surprised when adversity shows up...but we need to remember (and remind each other) that such challenges have their limits. Take responsibility for your failures, and move on. Adversity will be around only for a season; it has a beginning, and it will come to an end.

I heard PC once say that adversity is a great revealer: It doesn't always "make" the individual, but you can bet it will expose the true person within. Also, it tends to develop character, and while many of us may complain we have *plenty* of character already, adversity does indeed serve a great purpose. The truth is, we face battles daily. If you aren't experiencing any push-back, then you are not a threat to the enemy; basically, you're walking the wrong way. Think about it: The irony here is the more painful our lives, the better we're doing.

Years ago, I was given a valuable gift when I was told that when I was hurting, I should take my eyes off myself and go help someone in need—that it would not only benefit them, but it would change me in ways I never could have imagined. If we face trials with the right attitude, we'll find we can learn so much from them. Adversity not only reveals our need for God, but is a key way in which God teaches us. Scripture tells us repeatedly that God is faithful, and that He won't put more on us than we can bear. He won't necessarily prevent life's many forms of pain from touching us (though He could), but rather, with His loving guidance, will provide a way for us to endure it and, crazily, become better for it.

Most people focus on their problems and become blind to any solutions, but I know that God leverages all our painful moments for the better.

All those many rides home granted me a captive audience, and I did my best to take full advantage of every mile. One of the more memorable times was toward the end of the losing streak, when our players and parents were hungry for a win. We were getting closer now, like losing only by one or two runs in the last inning. (This was light years ahead of where we were a short month earlier, when our players did all they could just to string a hit or two together.) But our first victory was snatched out of our players' hands like a grade school bully making off with a kid's lunch money. Two outs in the last inning—so incredibly painful. That sad trip home afforded me the blessing of trying something new. I had just been reading the book of Ephesians, one of my favorites, and I started comparing the "Armor of God" to softball.

We talked about how the **Belt of Truth** could be used to cinch clothes, allowing freedom and movement, and also hold a warrior's sword. In some cases, the belt also could carry the player's/coach's playlist with bunts, steals, and hit and run plays. (I probably should have started with a different piece of armor first because, yeah, I was *really stretching* on finding that comparison, but it worked. Stay with me here.)

Next, we discussed the **Feet Shod with the Gospel of Peace**—that this is the Good News: "God forgives, then He gives." The Gospel takes hopeless beings and fills them with the eternity of Glory. We also compared this to our players' cleats—how they can carry the good news from base to base, how the spikes can dig in and help us stand our ground against unbelief.

The **Shield of Faith** guards against enemies and protects our spiritual lives even in the middle of trials. It allows us to block any impure thoughts or doubts that come our way, similar to the glove a player wears to protect against hard-hit balls in their direction.

The **Helmet of Salvation** serves a similar, protective purpose as a batting helmet: One protects our minds from outside forces and thoughts while the other protects our heads from a fast ball barreling toward us.

The **Sword of the Spirit** is the Word of God. Scripture is used to fight off arguments and attacks; it's meant to be used against your enemy. It's comparable to the player's bat and how that's used to fight off the opponent's nasty curve balls and belt-high fastballs.

The **Breastplate of Righteousness** covers the heart, lungs and other vital organs; without it, a soldier is completely vulnerable, asking for death. Without righteousness, we leave ourselves open to attack, but with it, we can fend off assaults on our hearts. This we likened to the team logo our athletes wear across their chests, and how we play for the person next to us. A soldier has no armor on their back side because the battle is in front of them; they are not expected to turn tail and retreat. The catcher has the same attire—helmet, chest protector, leg guards— and is expected to keep the battle in front of the plate, not at the back-stop.

As a coach, you never really know how any talk will be received, and this one was no different. I just hoped they heard what they needed to allow them to take the next steps in improving both their self-confidence and their walk with Christ. I do believe around this time they'd started to figure out that most of our talks merely used softball as a metaphor; they knew we were far more concerned that they created certain hab-its that would benefit them for years to come. You would think with as often as we'd lost there would be lots of finger-pointing and blame but, amazingly, there was none. A couple of players pulled me aside, though, saying they'd gotten a little discouraged and found themselves just going through the motions. They felt a few of them could put forth a little more effort, and I totally understood. Winning at anything can become habitual, *but so can losing*; if you aren't careful, you can develop a mentality of just doing enough to get by because it seems the outcome will be the same no matter what. This dangerous mentality can slither easily into everyday life, causing undue and unnecessary pain and dis-comfort. I try to relay to others to enjoy the journey, both the wins and (especially) the losses. **Both** are marvelous teachers.

During that losing season, we asked the players to shift their focus from winning to simply giving their best effort on each pitch, letting whatever was going to happen, happen. (It never mattered to me any-way; I was more concerned with creating a healthy habit of giving max-imum effort.) The pressure of getting their first win subsided, so they relaxed and really started to enjoy the process. But interestingly, that relaxed stance seemed to light a new fire in their eyes because they started to understand that getting blindsided by life can and will happen. They started to develop the courage that would fuel them to rise after life's blows and try again. Regardless of the end score, I felt so much more certain we were sending these athletes into the real world better prepared with the fortitude and will to get back in the game, no matter what.

Dealing with adversity means knowing you have a choice in your attitude, figuring out how to adjust your mindset, and donning the armor of God. If you've got the right foundation and understand that hurts and disappointments offer blessings in disguise, you'll be well-equipped to handle all life throws your way. I am not saying it won't hurt or be difficult; on the contrary, there will be tears sometimes. But if we can understand that adversity is temporary, this alone should give us hope. And we all know when a competitor has hope, the whole world had better watch out!

LEGENDS 99 EATING CRAWFISH IN STARKVILLE, MS

Chapter Ten

ON KNOWING WHAT TO CARRY

Imagine what you could do if you gave your goals everything you had. There are no statistics when it comes to success; people succeed when they make up their minds to do so. To succeed in any endeavor, there must be a sense of urgency. First, we start with a dream, which will help determine our destiny. But we must also be disciplined in our approach, and wise enough to know what should come with us, to achieve those dreams.

I got to see this in action a few summers back, when our team was playing in Ankeny, Iowa. They were hot and cold all week long; in one game, they looked as if no team could stay on the field with them, but in the next, you'd swear they were allergic to every aspect of the game of softball! It made zero sense; this was to be their last tournament before we moved up two age divisions, from 14U to 18U A, but the problem was that they were playing as if they needed to drop *down* two age divisions (along with going back to "C" class ball). They were just bogged down, and their body language and facial expressions revealed their frustration. They needed something, and we needed to give it to them… but what?

In an attempt to refocus their efforts, we reminded them they were born to win. Period. We talked about prioritizing their time and having tunnel vision, about having definite goals and eliminating distractions. The conversation was wide-ranging and fun, and the topics quickly evolved way past softball, like what to do with negative family and friends and how to make the most of their time each day. What we choose to do with those twenty-four is up to each one of us, and we'll prioritize what's most important to us. We also talked about having a close circle of influence and disregarding everyone and everything that distracts them from their goals. If we do what is easy, our lives will be hard, but if we do what is hard, our lives will become easy. People who are hungry for success do what others aren't willing to do. They are relentless, and they don't accept defeat. Hungry people have purpose...but we also noted that some things can get in the way of achieving everything we hope.

I shared that, a decade ago, Pastor Jason Kimbrow of New Life Church in North Little Rock gave me a profound image of what it means to live life when you're carrying what you shouldn't...things like generational curses (also known as family dysfunction), false guilt, fear, people-pleasing and more. I asked a player to come up, and started putting all our excess gear on her to show how such "emotional baggage" starts to wear us down. One duffel signified pride, another signified wounds from being hurt emotionally...and before long, she was doubled-over and unable to move. Most everyone carries scars and hurts of some kind, and when we go through life toting that baggage, life gets hard real quick.

When it comes to dealing with life's issues, most people avoid them until the pressures get to be too much, and they end up taking out their frustrations on the ones closest to them. But to move forward, we've got to decide whether we should carry the following.

Harsh Words: We have to be careful with what we say to others *and* ourselves. The adage "Sticks and stones may break my bones, but words will never hurt me" is garbage; some of our biggest scars come from harsh words spoken from one person to another. Words can be used to build a person up just as easily as they can take a person down to depths no one should ever experience.

Consider a bow and an arrow: I hunted a lot as a kid, and any person who has ever drawn back a bow knows as long as you don't release the arrow, all is fine. But the moment you release that arrow and it hits the intended target, irreparable damage is done. The same holds true regarding our words. As long as you are *thinking* and not *speaking*, everything is pretty much all right. But, once those words escape your lips and land in another person's ears, damage can be done. You can't un-say them, and the other person can't un-hear them. Saying we're sorry can fall flat; it's far better to guard our words before we ever speak.

Grudges: Humans tend to hold on to wrongs, replaying those hurts over and over until we've got them memorized. Ironically, we judge others by their actions but judge ourselves by our intentions. But holding grudges harms only us, holding us hostage, in effect. There's an old saying that holding on to resentments is like drinking rat poison while waiting for the rat to die. Such grudges are too much to carry: When we learn to forgive, we get freed from all bondage.

Generational Curses: This is one way of talking about family dysfunction and "the sins of the father." If we think, "My parents were drunks, so I will become a drunk," we're wrong. That doesn't have to be the case. But often we can be unaware of the weaknesses that get passed down the line; just like a certain disease can "run in the family," so can tendencies toward blaming, avoiding responsibility, being rigid in our thinking and more. If we're willing to have our eyes opened, God will gently correct us so that such generational curses end with us in *our* generation.

Pride: This is another relationship-killer. The pastor said if you live with pride, those closest to you will know it…but they won't tell you because, if they did, you'd deny it anyway! It's an interesting balance—that is, being humble enough to allow others to speak into our lives but not so needy that we're hanging on their every word. Do you resist others speaking into your life? Be humble and admit your mistakes. If you completely resist others' perceptions and opinions, you may need to look at why those are so hard to hear; you can't approach the cross with pride in your heart. *And*...you also don't want to be held captive to others' affirmations. If you feel too prideful for gaining their "favor," you'll end up doing things for the wrong reasons and experiencing unintended consequences.

Envy (ours and others'): We're told explicitly in Scripture not to compare ourselves to others—what they do, what they have—but envy is an extremely common (and destructive) emotion. How easy is it to compare and find ourselves wanting? But this particular "bag" manages to steal our joy twice—once when we feel we've gotten the short end of the stick, and once when we covet others' perceived bounties. For us, the quickest way past envy is an attitude of gratitude, thankful for everything we have.

"But What About Me?" Thinking: It's true that not everyone wants to see you succeed. Some people actually revel in others' failures. It's what we Southerners call the "Crabs in a Bucket" Syndrome. Ever heard of it? Allow me to explain: If you put one crab in a bucket, it stands a decent chance of getting out, but if you put two or more in the same bucket, most if not all will perish. The reasoning is that as one crab reaches toward the top, the others grab ahold and drag him back down. Humans are similar in that most don't want others to succeed if they can't also. They will do everything in their power to destroy the ambitions of others who want to improve themselves, but this pouty, put-upon mindset only keeps them feeling perpetually victimized.

Imagine going through life allowing others to see the bags you are carrying: Which weights are straining you? We reminded our girls that all those unnecessary things we drag around every day—hurt and pride and so much more—God longs to carry for us. If you walk in faith daily, when it comes time for the Lord's help, you won't have to search for His number.

In Matthew 11:28-30, Jesus says, "Come to me, all you who are weary and burdened, and I will give you rest. Take my yoke upon you and learn from me, for I am gentle and humble in heart, and you will find rest for your souls. For my yoke is easy and my burden is light" (NIV). The yoke here can refer to the wooden implement a farmer uses to guide an ox, but it also can refer to a rabbi's teaching. Back in Jesus' time, if a rabbi agreed to teach a student, the pupil took on that rabbi's "yoke"—that is, how the teacher interpreted the Scriptures—and some yokes were "heavier" (more rule-based) than others. Here, Jesus is saying we don't need to strain under the weight of all that excess, but rather that He's got a pretty simple life-plan to follow: Love Him, love others, love ourselves. But we can't do that when we're carrying stuff we shouldn't.

I wish I could say our players came back and won the tournament, but they didn't. They played only average that weekend, and we were put out early and headed for home. But I know that talk made an impact, because it gave the team a chance to see their coaches as humans who dealt with the same struggles. In fact, that talk allowed me to explain some of the baggage I carried for over two decades....of feeling worthless at times, of not living up to expectations, of doing things for the wrong reasons. I was able to share honestly how I confronted my baggage, turned it over and released it. And traveling lighter has made all the difference.

If the world tells you that you aren't good enough, get a second opinion. The more you remain in conversation with God throughout the day, the more available you will find Him, and the clearer it will be about what you should pick up...and what you should set down.

ME AND HANNAH

Chapter Eleven

ON THE LONGEST RIDE HOME

Teach us to number our days, that we may gain a heart of wisdom.
–Psalm 90:12 (NIV)

"Did you fill up her car? Did you check her tires?" Dana asked me.
"Yes and yes," I replied.

"Did you load her luggage?" And then: "Hannah, make sure you close the door to your room."

Her room. I knew Dana was talking to me and I answered, but honestly, I didn't really know what I said nor what she asked. I saw her mouth moving, but never heard a word. As the mom, Dana was in organizational mode; I, however, was in a haze, because this day was never supposed to come.

Her room. All I could think about was the day we realized Hannah was left-handed, when she picked up a plastic bat at the age of three and put the ball on a tee and let it rip. She probably hit five or six balls before we even realized she was hitting from the left side, each time running the imaginary bases from home to home. It didn't matter she ran past them the wrong way, it was just entertaining to watch.

Her room. That soon-to-be-empty room that housed her young lifetime of memories, where hurts were soothed and wounds were mended. It was a place where we discussed life and prepared for the future.

Well: *One* of us did. And one of us, right now, was struggling.

All I have ever wanted was a family—a wife and kids. And now, it

93

seemed that was being taken away or broken apart bit by bit. I felt as helpless as a man on a raft in the middle of the Pacific Ocean, and I couldn't do anything about it.

It was time for my baby girl to leave.

It was her room still—a strangely clean room, though, one I wished still had an unmade bed and clothes on the floor. One in which you couldn't open the closet door because a pile of clean clothes had it blocked...clothes that were supposed to have been put away but were lodged so tightly against the door that you could barely peek inside.

What I wouldn't give to have her room look like that again...

Where did it all go? How did the time slip away? I'm so excited for her and her future, and witnessing her being on the cusp of her dream of playing college softball, but my heart... My heart seems to be breaking at the same time. Anyone whose child has left home can relate. I kept asking myself, *Did I tell her often enough that I love her? Did we prepare her for what she is about to face?* But the main question that kept rolling around was, *Why can't we have more time?*

"Make sure Maggie is locked up, Hayden. We need to get on the road," Dana instructed. "Turn off the living room lights, but make sure the outside lights are on. You know I like to come home to a house that's lit on the outside."

I looked at Dana and wondered, *Am I the only one fazed by this?* How do others do this? I shut and locked the door and, just like that, we started a new chapter in the book of Hurst. Hayden and I took the truck while Dana rode with Hannah in her car. The trip to college should have lasted about two hours, but it seemed to take about fifteen minutes. There wasn't much conversation between us; I think he knew I needed time to think and just be. While he had his earbuds in listening to a mixture of Johnny Cash, Toby Mac, and Van Halen, I sat quietly. My mind works overtime while I am driving. I can't explain why, but thoughts just seem a little clearer on the road. I feel I can articulate better, and ideas tend to flow freely when I'm traveling. Some need a quiet room to formulate their thoughts; I just need the comforting hum of rubber on blacktop... but even that couldn't lessen the ache I felt inside.

As we pulled onto the campus, it felt like we'd just left our small town of Elkins, and I could swear my coffee was still hot enough to burn the roof of my mouth. My emotions took over, so I had to remind myself to take a moment and do what I tell my players when times get a little rough: *I had to Cowboy Up.* I had to remind myself that this was no punishment, but rather what she'd worked so hard for. All those days after practice—the hitting in the cage, the soft toss on the field, the countless hours working on technique while hitting off the tee—set her up to achieve this goal. I was supposed to be happy, but it was happiness tinged with sadness…and I didn't know that was even possible.

I have faced adversity before, but this was on a whole 'nother level. This felt like being in the boxing ring with Mike Tyson while blindfolded and allowed to only use your off hand. I needed help, and lots of it. I found it in Proverbs 3:5-6: *Trust in the Lord with all your heart and lean not on your own understanding; in all your ways submit to Him, and He will make your paths straight* (NIV), and again in Psalm 46:10: *Be still and know that I am God* (ESV).

I must have recited those verses in my head a thousand times that day.

I don't remember much about unloading the truck and filling Hannah's dorm room with what seemed to me like a boatload of memories and an enormous piece of my heart. What I do recall is how she interacted and bonded practically instantaneously with her new teammates. Eventually the time came to say our goodbyes, and we headed back to the truck. As I looked back at the dorm where my little girl stood, I saw instead a poised, eighteen-year-old young woman with the world at her fingertips. I kept looking back, hoping to catch a glimpse of the five-year-old in pigtails, riding her pink scooter up and down our driveway, but it was not to be. That time had come and gone. What I have left of those days is held in a plastic bin in the closet—images frozen on film—and in the annals of my mind.

Preachers say that God won't give us more than we can handle—heck, even I have used that line several times when counseling others—but at that moment, it felt like God was pushing His limits and testing mine.

For as short as the ride *to* college seemed, that ride home felt like it took forever. I was officially out of tears, or at least that's how I felt. It was so bittersweet: When I'd lost my joy in coaching several years back, these kids helped me find it again. I would always get excited when it was time to head to practice because it was *our time*. The practice field was a fifty-five-minute trip from our front door to the complex in Gentry, Arkansas. The kids dreaded the drive but not me, no, sir. I cherished every mile and minute. I looked forward to practice days, but it wasn't because I enjoyed the heat and the sweat: It was because I got to spend two whole hours in a vehicle with just me and Hannah, or me and Hayden. During those rides, we talked about school, dreams, life, love, and Christ. We talked about becoming better people in spite of how others treated us. We discussed doing what is right, especially when it's hard. We touched upon unconditional love and forgiveness, and how God loves us just as much as He loves the world's greatest…and the least. We had conversations about giving our best and doing things before being asked, because it just means more. And we talked about finding our gifts but, more importantly, helping others recognize theirs, and doing our part to make this world a better place.

The kids thought they were just heading to practice, but those hours cemented my family. Sometimes you will never know the value of a moment until it becomes a memory.

Our children cannot understand the value of such time until, perhaps, they have children of their own. But as we age, we understand life is an uphill climb, but the higher we get, the better the view tends to be. For me, the seemingly endless drives gave me a glimpse of what could be, enabled me to develop strong young adults and leaders, and provided quality time with my kids, without distractions.

As our children leave the nest, parents the world over pray we taught them what they need to know to make it. I feel especially lucky that I had all those extra hours to get to know my children, and connect with them on a personal level—that made every mile special and provided memories that the years cannot erase. Time has a way of showing us what really matters. And even as I struggle to let my little girl go, I keep close to my heart all those smiles and tears, the times and talks, and know that my children—and I—are so, so much better for them.

The rides home, no matter how long, were simply…priceless.

(L TO R) TAYLOR HULL, HANNAH HURST AND JADYN HEINLE
LEAVING THE PARK AFTER THEIR LAST GAME AS LEGENDS

Chapter Twelve

ON THE LAST TIME

And just like that…*Poof!* It's over. Where did the time go? Because, oh… how I wish I could have it back! I received so much joy from watching these kids compete, far more than I ever did when I myself played. What leaders they have become! Always encouraging and putting others before themselves, leading by example, doing the right thing…they are my heroes because of the examples they have set.

If it had to end, well, then, they ended it the best way they could: Giving their teammates, coaches, and fans the utmost respect. They honored the game by leaving it all out on the field, every time. They approached each game, each pitch, as though it was their last. People noticed. They earned their opponents' respect by simply playing the game the correct way, the way it was meant to be played.

This ride has been an emotional roller coaster. I listened as my childhood friend, Pam (Nichols) Gulledge, spoke about her daughter, Anna Beth, at the end of senior year:

For the last fifteen years, we have told our children to get up and get ready for school. Today, we said that for the last time. I could barely get those words out of my mouth before the tears started forming. The last time…the last time. There seems to be so many of those lately. Tears formed again as we drove into the complex's parking lot, not knowing if this trip would be the last time I would ever watch her play softball. The game alone almost did me in.

We have been extremely fortunate over the years to have had employers who encouraged us to attend those special activities for our children. For that, I will be forever grateful. Once those moments are gone, they are just that—gone. You can't put the toothpaste back in the tube, nor can you get a do-over. Outsiders would say we were putting our hobbies and what we wanted to do on the back burner while we chased our kids around. Guess what? We have no regrets. I'm glad we missed out on that television show we loved to watch. I'm ok that we missed going to bed early and getting plenty of sleep. I'm glad we missed those home-cooked meals and replaced them with late night bowls of cereal. It was totally worth it to be able to make those memories because I knew that one day, it would be the last time. It's the end of an era as they say. Looking around tonight, I saw all the parents with little kids and thought, "That was us just a few short years ago." Where did the time go?

Things are a little different now versus how it was for me growing up in the '70s and '80s. When I played, there were distinct seasons: Football was played in the fall, basketball in the winter, and baseball in the spring and summer. Now, it seems each sport is available all year long in some form or fashion. As anyone who's performed a task or job for years at a time can attest, there is a fine line between loving it and feeling burned out by it. Having dealt with burnout at my job on several occasions, I have found that, at least for me, it is best cured by walking barefoot on the sand in August or sitting in a tree stand on a cool November afternoon.

When a kid plays travel ball on a competitive level, both player and parent sacrifice. They both risk burnout. While most kids spend the summer at the pool or lake, ballplayers are polishing their skills at practice or games. You practice two or three times a week and spend your weekends in hotel rooms and ballparks. In our age of social media, where events and goings-on are instantly visible for anyone to see, some teens can feel like they're missing out on the normal rites of passage, which can turn "love" to "loathe" to "resentment" when it comes to such a stringent playing schedule. And when love reaches resentment in anything, much less a sport, trying to have a reasonable conversation about the matter pretty much falls on deaf ears.

I am reminded of a situation that took place a few seasons ago with one of my players. Her parents struggled with the possibility that their kid didn't want to play softball any longer. Unbeknownst to them, this feeling had been gathering steam for some time, and it had come to a head the weekend prior. Her parents asked me to spend some time with her at a restaurant in their hometown and see whether she would open up and share why this sudden change had occurred.

What I didn't know was that she had no idea it would just be the two of us talking. "Awkward" doesn't do this encounter justice. I spent the first twenty minutes or so just trying to chip away at the rock-hard exterior that she had so quickly constructed.

I felt I first had to let her know I understood where she was coming from. I was dealing with the same situation in my own household— my own daughter felt she was missing out on special moments with her non-softball playing friends. Then, second, she had to hear I was not there to talk her into playing. I had her back, and I told her so. If, after our conversation, she didn't want to continue playing, I would stand in the gap with her when it came to her family. The only thing I required was that we have an honest, open conversation about the pros and cons alongside her dreams and goals. Just a few months earlier, we talked about her interest in playing for several universities; that alone helped me feel her love for the game was still there inside. The challenge would be chipping away at her façade long and hard enough to reach the root of her change of heart.

Eventually, she opened up and gave me a few examples as to why she felt as she did, like missing swimming parties, dates, movies, and time hanging out with her friends—all that simply being a teenager entailed. In her mind, she would never get those opportunities and events back. Of course I understood: High school comes around only once. She extended me the courtesy of taking the opposing view...one that could have been the catalyst to quickly reconstructing that newly torn-down wall. I talked about the reasons to continue—her love for the game itself and her ability to further her education while playing in college. More importantly, I gently pointed out that maybe her thought process was somewhat one-sided; she was focused on what she felt she was missing but didn't see what she had gained. I believe we all have a tendency to do that, focusing on what we don't have and taking for granted what we do. It's all a matter of perspective.

She'd worked hard; honestly, they all had. She had tucked away all the little things she'd experienced with her teammates, like hunting crabs late at night on the beaches of Gulf Shores, Alabama; traveling to towns and states she might have never visited; building new friendships; playing cards and Spoons in hotel meeting rooms until well after midnight; and, most importantly, creating life-long memories and enjoying a stronger bond with her parents. We talked about shifting her focus just a bit; she knew that once she decided to quit, there would be no going back to capture those last few years of high school and travel ball. Once it's gone, it's gone…and she didn't want to be thirty or fifty or more years old, wondering what might have been or what she might have accomplished. That kind of reflecting can gnaw at people, making their latter days in life pretty darn uncomfortable.

One other great concern of mine was that once people leave a somewhat structured environment and become a product of their own devices, they can easily be influenced by their new surroundings—positively or negatively. Proverbs 13:20 says, *Walk with the wise and become wise, for a companion of fools suffers harm* (NIV). I had seen this happen before with one of my most talented baseball players; his senior year had him on track to be drafted in the later rounds at best, or be invited to visit three major league clubs at worst. As the coach who had introduced him to the game of baseball at age eight and who had worked tirelessly at helping develop his skills, I was unbelievably excited for him. But what I didn't know was that he had started running with a different crowd, the kind that parents use as an example to warn their kids. Eventually, the pull of his peers was greater than the possibilities of what could be. He started skipping practices, then games, and the next thing you know, he became Exhibit A of *What Not to Do*. It was heartbreaking to watch, and it took several years before he made his way back—years that couldn't be retrieved. It bothers me even to this day. I often wonder what I might have done to help prevent his downfall, but I've reached the painful conclusion that it was *his* journey to travel, and I was merely a spectator along for the uneasy ride.

Now, I'm not suggesting that this young woman would have taken a similar route, but I knew she had more to offer. And I won't lie: I really wanted her to continue to play. But most of all, I wanted her happiness; she was pained, and it showed. But she soon came to realize that the pain that she was experiencing then was nothing compared to what it would have felt like to quit.

Having such "real" conversations is hard, but the discomfort is so worth it. As I rode home from the restaurant that day, I realized there will always be a conflict between good and good enough, so we need to prepare our minds to receive the best that life has to offer. And we simply need to stay in the game, because we never know which time will be the last time.

It's hard to put into words the feelings I experienced as we exchanged text messages long after that fateful meeting, on the day she signed her National Letter of Intent to play softball in college.

It's hard to express how happy and proud I am as your coach. I am excited for you and your journey in becoming all that God has called you to be. My prayer for you is that you keep God first in everything you do, put others second, and keep yourself third. Always look for ways to give back, and you will have more than you have ever dreamed. Don't take for granted this opportunity you have been given and, lastly, enjoy the ride. Take time to notice life's little victories. Today seems a lifetime ago from the Mexican restaurant in Gentry, Arkansas. No matter how hard life seems to get at times, remember, God is in control. KEEP SWINGING!

Thank you, Coach! I can't express how thankful I am to have had the opportunity to play for you. I've not only become a better athlete, but I also feel like I have become a better person. Thank you for coaching me, not only on the team but also throughout life!

In Mark 9:23, Jesus says, "…All things are possible for one who believes" (ESV). It doesn't say some things, it says **ALL** things! I believe in my players. They believe in me. We believe in the love of a good game and the love of a great God. For all our coaches and players and parents, these days have been a gift…and we've learned to celebrate them for as long as we have them.

ANNA KIDD, HANNAH HURST, TAYLOR HULL & BROOKE BOSTON
AFTER WINNING IN OKLAHOMA CITY, OK

Afterword
ON HAVING A DREAM TO CHASE

I often tell my children to identify their dreams and to go after them like they owe them money...to chase them with everything they've got. I relay the same message to my ballplayers. Life is tough, but it is way tougher without dreams.

I believe if we give our dreams over to God, we can rest in knowing He will watch over us as we help bring them to life. 1 John 5:14-15 reads, *This is the confidence we have in approaching God: that if we ask anything according to His will, He hears us. And if we know that He hears us—whatever we ask—we know that we have what we asked of Him* (NIV).

It is our formal request, giving our prayers strength. We present back to God what He's already said, and ask Him to honor what He's already promised in His Word. God's Word is His will. He instructs us to return His Word back to him, but for us to do that, we first must know what His book says.

We can approach Him confidently: "Lord, you said in your Word that You would meet all my needs according to the riches of His glory in Christ Jesus (Philippians 4:19). I am presenting Your Word back to You because in Isaiah 55:11, You said, 'So shall my word be that goes out from my mouth; it shall not return to me empty, but it shall accomplish that which I purpose, and shall succeed in the thing for which I sent it'" (ESV).

I encourage parents and children alike to chase their dreams with a vigor unmatched by any other. It's never too late. In Mark 11:23-24,

Jesus says, "Truly, I tell you, if anyone says to this mountain, 'Go, throw yourself into the sea,' and does not doubt in their heart but believes that what they say will happen, it will be done for them. Therefore I tell you, whatever you ask for in prayer, believe that you have received it, and it will be yours" (NIV).

I, too, have dreams…dreams of making a difference in others' lives, dreams of being a good husband and father, dreams of becoming a true friend and counselor. But I also have a more tangible dream—a dream of a faith-based sports complex complete with baseball, softball and football fields. I want it to also contain tennis and basketball courts, a sand volleyball pit, a walking trail and a kid's play area. It will have a walkway from the entrance to the middle of the complex, where three flagpoles will be planted: One for the American flag, one for the Arkansas flag, and one for the Christian flag. They will all be nestled close to a cross upon which people can nail their concerns, cares, prayers, and dreams, knowing others will be there to pray over them. I envision paths leading away from the cross to different fields or courts, with signs displaying positive affirmations and Scripture firmly staked along each path and walking trail.

My dream is to have a place where high schools, colleges, and travel/rec teams all are welcome. It will be open for practices and games, or just for teams to come and tour. It will allow me to host team camps that bring in speakers to breathe life into athletes, their families, and anyone else within earshot. As players practice or play, my goal is that not only will they be impacted by such a positive setting, but their family members could walk the grounds and be filled by positive affirmations and God's Word.

I believe we will have this facility, because God placed it on my heart eight years ago while I was living in North Little Rock. It was as plain as day. I believe this is my calling, and my calling is to make a real difference, just as I witnessed on all those precious rides home here on Earth… and what I hope to experience after my final ride home to heaven.

How I long to hear I was a good and faithful servant!

How will it happen? That's not my job to know. My job is to take the steps in faith, believing and trusting that God will follow through on His promises. The "how," well…that's up to God. Here is what I *do* know: We as a society have strayed far from God and His Word. In this world of ever-compromised "principles," we could all use a barrel full of positive. I think we all could use a place where as kids play and practice, they also have the opportunity to hear the Good News and to come across God's Word. This is one way to help change this ol' world.

For where two or three gather in my name, there am I with them (Matthew 18:20, NIV).

Who will believe with me? Will you?

We endure only to achieve.
We accomplish only to push harder.
We have will without limits.
Enough is never too much.
We are defined by our character…
We come from every walk of life,
Often remaining unnoticed…..UNTIL NOW!
-Unknown

Contact

To book Keith for corporate events, speaking engagements, school organizations, or team talks, call 479-422-3367 or email keithhurst14@gmail.com.